The Craft
of Copywriting

Alastair Crompton's films and press work have been honored by highly prestigious advertising awards. He's been associated with many first-class ad agencies, including Doyle Dane Bernbach in the United Kingdom in the position of deputy creative director. Mr. Crompton now works on a free-lance basis from his home in England.

54

THE CRAFT OF COPY-WRITING

How to Write Great Copy that Sells

ALASTAIR CROMPTON

A SPECTRUM BOOK

PRENTICE-HALL, INC., ENGLEWOOD CLIFFS, NEW JERSEY 07632

Library of Congress Cataloging in Publication Data

CROMPTON, ALASTAIR.
    The craft of copywriting.

    "A Spectrum Book."
    Includes index.
    1.   Advertising copy.   I.   Title.
HF5825.C7   1982   659.13′22   82-7647
ISBN 0-13-188409-3   AACR2
ISBN 0-13-188391-7 (pbk.)

10   9   8   7   6   5   4   3   2   1

ISBN 0-13-188409-3

ISBN 0-13-188391-7 (PBK.)

Editorial/production supervision by Carol Smith
Cover design and interior design by Jeannette Jacobs
Manufacturing buyer: Cathie Lenard

This Spectrum Book is available to businesses and organizations
at a special discount when ordered in large quantities.
For information, contact Prentice-Hall, Inc., General Publishing Division,
Special Sales, Englewood Cliffs, N.J. 07632.

Prentice-Hall International, Inc., *London*
Prentice-Hall of Australia Pty. Limited, *Sydney*
Prentice-Hall Canada Inc., *Toronto*
Prentice-Hall of India Private Limited, *New Delhi*
Prentice-Hall of Japan, Inc., *Tokyo*
Prentice-Hall of Southeast Asia Pte. Ltd., *Singapore*
Whitehall Books Limited, *Wellington, New Zealand*

To Jill

Contents

CONTENTS

Foreword

On the second page of Alastair Crompton's book, I found myself hunting for a pencil to underline what struck me as an especially wise sentence. Then I found myself underlining another sentence on the third page, and another on the fourth, and a whole paragraph on page eight. When I finished *The Craft of Copywriting*, I found that I'd decorated almost the whole book.

This is an intelligent and practical book, and great fun to read. Mr. Crompton never succumbs to jargon. You won't find him using the pretentious word "positioning" even once. What you will find is a lot of good advice that should help you in your work. A lot more good advice, I may add, than you'd get in most advertising "courses." The chapters on "How to judge your work" and "How to defend your artwork" are worth their weight in gold.

One of my favorite sentences turns up in the chapter titled "The creative director." It reads, *"The creative director is the one man in the agency whose work it is easy to assess."* Of course! There it all is—advertising he's written himself, advertising written by other people that he's *approved*—spread out on the printed page, or on the nineteen-inch-screen, for all the world to *see*. But if that's what you'd like to be—*The Craft of Copywriting* would be a pretty good place to begin.

Reva Korda
Chairman, Korda Rand Levine Inc.

XV

Preface

This book is written for anyone who wants to know how advertisements are made. You may be a student taking a course in advertising. You may be studying at a university, wondering whether a writing job in an advertising agency is something you could, or would like to, do. You may have already joined an agency as a trainee and want to know a little about the creative side of the business. You may be a young copywriter who wonders if this book has anything to tell him.

You may be an established copywriter interested in how a colleague sees the business. You may be a brand manager, keen to understand better the creative work presented to you. Or you may have nothing to do with advertising at all and are just trying to find out if there is any truth in the talk about hidden persuaders and mind manipulating and whether there are secret techniques used to sell the public goods it doesn't want, at prices it can't afford.

If you are any of those people, you'll get something from this book. Its special aim, however, is to turn would-be copywriters into very good copywriters who will find themselves in demand and able to earn a good living. If it means that more people produce intelligent advertising and that more companies get better value for their money from their agencies, or if it helps you to be happy and make money in the job you have chosen to do, it will have been worthwhile.

note on the illustrations

This book is illustrated with 21 advertisements, produced by some of the best advertising agencies in London and New York. As a copywriter, I may have been heard to say that the most important part of any advertisement is the headline. But the illustrations have been chosen because of their pictures. (This explains why I've given the art directors a credit, but not the various copywriters).

The advertisement opposite was created by Doyle Dane Bernbach agency in New York, and has appeared in Britain, France, Germany, and Belgium, as well as the United States. It happened when art director Charles Piccirillo, who wasn't even working on VW at the time, approached writer Bob Levenson with the cartoon of a man holding a gas pump nozzle to his head. "I'm not sure what it means," said Piccirillo, "but I think it's funny." "I'm not sure what it means either," replied Levenson, "but it ought to say, 'Or buy a Volkswagen.'"

It's a perfect example of art and copy working together. The picture is, in fact, doing more than half the work. Without the picture, the headline would make no sense.

When you first begin to learn the craft of copywriting, you tend to think the words should carry the brunt of the sales pitch. The advertisements shown in this book demonstrate that isn't always so. They also demonstrate another point: A headline that says only what you can see from the picture is working at half strength.

I have not set out to pick the best ads of the decade. Some of the work included has been commended by the judges of creative work, but most of it has passed without any recognition from any award-giving body. Yet every ad is an excellent piece of craftsmanship that has earned its place here because it can teach you something. So when you come to them, look at the advertisements to see what techniques they use, because it is by understanding those that you will help yourself to do better work.

Acknowledgments   I would like to express my thanks to the following people for help I received in producing the American edition of this book. To Reva Korda of Korda Rand Levine Inc. for writing the Foreword although she didn't know me from Adam. To Robert H. Levenson of Doyle Dane Bernbach Inc., for helping me choose the American advertisements shown. And to Teresa E. McVeigh (also of DDB) for persuading all the advertisers to let me use their work, and providing all the names of the art directors so that credit could be given where it is due. They are living proof, if it were needed, that when it comes to creative work, nobody does it on his own.

Or buy a Volkswagen.

The Craft
of Copywriting

Your First Day in the Creative Department

Advertising agencies need four kinds of people: account people, media people, production people, and creative people. The first three kinds have no place in this book, although you will find them wandering in and out of its pages. But we can't have you sitting in your office the first day without knowing who is likely to walk in, so let us begin with the briefest description of what account, media, and production people do.

Account people are the ones with nice suits, nice haircuts, and nice accents. Their job is to represent the agency to the client, and the client to the agency. They help the client to think through every aspect of selling his product. They carry reports of the client's needs to the agency, and they carry the work the agency produces to the client. They are, in a word, the contact people. Of course, a good account person is primarily a businessman able to understand and make recommendations on every aspect of selling. Generally speaking, it is an account person who is the chairman or managing director of the agency.

You're unlikely to start work on any advertisement unless you have first been briefed by an account person. An account person knows the client, understands his business, and should have virtually all the facts about it at his fingertips. Account people want to be loved, they want creative people to be able to think clearly and work very fast, and they do not want to be shouted at. You will be a more successful copywriter if you learn to like them.

Media people also wear nice suits, but they are occasionally seen with their jackets and ties off. It is their job to know all about, and to tell you all about, newspapers, television, magazines, posters, and radio—in fact, any medium where your advertisement could appear. They should know who reads, looks at, and listens to the various media and how you can reach the most people the most often and the most effectively for the least money. Sometimes media people can be very imaginative; if you find an imaginative media person, grapple him to thy soul with hoops of steel. He can make an idea you have communicate better and faster simply by suggesting the appropriate medium for it.

Production people do not always wear nice suits and are frequently seen in sweaters, T-shirts, or sports jackets and jeans. This in no way affects their efficiency; in fact, it has been argued that the more relaxed they are in their dress, the better they are able to concentrate on the job they have to do. This argument is also put forward to explain why creative people often look very scruffy.

The production person's job is to take the advertisement you have made and handle it in such a way that it can be reproduced on a poster or in a newspaper or magazine. Production people understand what will and will not look good when it is printed, and they should be listened to if they tell you that your advertisement is going to look like a disaster. They will advise you how small you can make a photograph before it becomes indecipherable on coarse newsprint. They will talk to printers and encourage them to reproduce faithfully the colors in a transparency. They are happy to make suggestions on what should be retouched in order to print with clarity.

In my experience, production people are willing and cheerful; and if you speak to them as colleagues, there is little they will not do for you. They also have access to a stream of weekly and monthly magazines that often reach their offices before they reach the stands, and for copies of which your spouse will be very grateful. Copywriters should never get on the wrong side of production people because they rely on them for the proofs of their work, which go to make up a writer's portfolio.

the creative types

Now that you know the three kinds of people (apart from creative people) who, if you have landed in a friendly agency, might knock on your door and introduce themselves, it is time to talk about creative people. The creative person who will be closest to you every day of your working life will be your art director. An art director, as the name suggests, directs the way an advertisement looks. He lays it out, decides what should be in the picture, supervises the photograph or drawing if there is one, decides on the appropriate type face, the size and positioning of the logotype (client's name block), and how big the body text should be. You may work solely with one art director, or you may work with several on different accounts, depending on the system operating in your agency. It doesn't really matter, as long as you actually *work with* an art director. There was a time when copywriters sat in one department, wrote their words, and then sent them through the messenger boy to the art directors sitting in another department. The problem with this was that it overlooked the simple fact that two heads are better than one. Two creative people working to make an advertisement are likely to make it quicker and better if they swop headlines and ideas. So although you may have an office of your own, you should always be willing to leave it and join your art director in his office. If you are both sitting together anyway, so much the better, although there are some writers who prefer a cubbyhole to themselves as (they say) it helps them to think about the body text of their advertisement and pound away on their typewriters without disturbing anyone.

There are other kinds of creative people besides art directors, and one you should get to know early is the television producer. A good TV and film producer is worth his weight in gold medals. Even if you choose the production company and director you want to make the film, the agency producer, if he is doing his job properly, will help you make sure that the idea you have in your mind is the one that ends up on the screen. He will also be able to tell you, if you have a wild, crazy idea, whether it is practicable. He will know at first glance whether your script contains too many words for the length of a film or radio commercial. If he is a professional, he will be able to "see" the commercial before it is made and know whether it's going to work or not.

The television producer also takes care of all the boring but important details of TV work. He OKs the bills, books the artists, reserves recording studios, plans trips if you're off on location, and does a dozen things that—if they weren't looked after—would spell disaster. Make friends with your television producer and do not get on your high horse if he dares to comment on your scripts. He may not be able to write them himself, any more than you can write, say, a pop song, but he should be allowed a view as to whether he likes them or not.

the typographer

Another creative person who'll help you is the agency typographer, the man who knows how best to suit the type face to the message. He's the man who, to take an extreme example, if your headline says GIVE A DAMN, will not let you set it in script or, if it says ANGELS OF MERCY, is unlikely to recommend a heavy black sans serif face. He can also tell you how much room a given number of words will take up. He will recommend complimentary faces, so that the body text does not look out of place with the headline. He will help with adaptations to larger or smaller spaces. And if you take him to lunch and get him talking, he's likely to spellbind you with stories about the history of type.

If you are lucky, your agency will have an illustrator. He's the person who takes your advertisement after you've thought of it and draws it up so you can present it to the client. The one thing he must be able to do is draw, but the best illustrators should be able to read your mind; and if you want the baby in the picture to have a particular smile, or the housewife to have a certain expression, he should be able to capture it for you. It calls for a deftness of touch and a skill to create impressions without over-working the picture, and the best illustrators soon leave advertising agencies and work freelance, where they can earn a lot more money. Illustrators may also decide to become art directors and thereby enjoy the thrill of initiating ideas, whereas illustrators have to interpret the ideas of other people.

the chief and the indians

There are two other kinds of creative people we haven't yet talked about: the creative director and the people who do the finished artwork in the agency studio. The creative director you will have already met. He's the one who interviewed you and gave you the job. His role is one of the most important in the agency and because, if you are a good writer, you may one day be a creative director yourself, I have given him a chapter to himself. The studio manager and the paste-up artists are also worth making friends with. Their job is to communicate with the production people, preparing the finished artwork so that your advertisements can be printed. They need patience, a sense of design, and a keen eye; and if they do their job properly, they can save the agency a lot of money and you a lot of heartache. If they do their job badly, they can lose everyone a fortune.

don't just sit there, do something

All right—there you are sitting at your desk, and you know who might come and visit you. What do you need before you can start work? You need a chair you feel comfortable in, pulled up to a desk you feel comfortable at. You need a layout pad and some thin and thick felt-tip pens. You need a typewriter and typing paper. Some copywriters say that they cannot work straight onto a typewriter. First, they can't type and, second, they find the habit of writing in longhand helps them think and lets them go back to cross words out without the palaver of pushing reverse keys. If you haven't made up your mind one way or the other, my advice is to work *with* a typewriter. The fact that you find it hard to type to start with will make you think twice about every word before you put it down. Gradually, you will get the feel of the number of words you have written, and this will help you economize on words and avoid writing too much. And last, you won't have to stand over your secretary when she is typing the finished version, apologizing for your terrible writing. But I should make it clear that the typewriter doesn't come into the act until you are writing the body copy. And before that, you and the art director must have thought of the theme and pictures that will make up the advertisement. In other words, you have to have had the idea.

Most young copywriters also start off with three books: a dictionary, Roget's *Thesaurus*, and a dictionary of quotations. A straight dictionary, I agree, is essential, but in all my time as a copywriter, I can't remember a single occasion when Roget or the dictionary of quotations was of any help whatever. Neither of them ever gave me the faintest advertising idea.

Where you *will* get a lot of help, however, is from the agency library. (If your agency hasn't got one, then spend 10 minutes on the streets until you've found the nearest public library.) Introduce yourself to the person in charge and let him or her know that you are a copywriter, that you have to produce advertisements, and that, in your work, you can never have too many facts. And that you intend to be in and out of the library, checking and finding out things, for as long as you belong to the agency. Good library people are never happier than when their resources are being stretched, and, provided you always return whatever stuff they lend you, you'll never have a problem.

A good agency library has a section on statistics where you should be able to find out facts, such as how many airlines or railways there are in the world, how many people in New York own color television sets, and so on. It also, generally, has a set of *Encyclopaedia Brittanicas*, which have many times provided the spice that made my body copy appetizing. I once had the job of writing 10 consecutive half-page advertisements in a magazine, each one featuring a bottle of fizzy mixer drink (tonic, ginger ale, soda, and so on). It was clear to me that I could never fill 10 half-pages with interesting stuff about mixers; on the other hand, stories and lore about drinking have filled books. A few minutes in the library and I found the reminiscences of the head bartender to a top hotel. There was enough meat there to make 10 half-pages relevant and riveting.

go to the pictures

The next thing you should do is telephone the agency screening room and ask them to show you the agency reel. The agency reel, for those who don't know, is a selection of the latest film and television commercials the agency has produced—ones of which it is most proud. It is most frequently wheeled out and shown to prospective clients when the agency is pitching for new business. Watching the agency reel will do two things: First, it will get you familiar with the clients in the agency who use the screening room and, second, it will show you the general standard of agency creative work to give you an idea of what you have to live up to.

If you haven't already got one, you should get a list of *all* the clients the agency has. You will most certainly have been told those clients whose accounts you will be expected to work on. Go to the production manager and ask if you can borrow the proof books of your accounts. The proof books (again for those who don't know) contain a record of every newspaper and magazine advertisement that has ever been prepared for that particular company while it has been a client of your agency. It is a history of that company's press advertising. You can have an enjoyable time just following the various themes that have been used, and they should, ideally, have one overall tone of voice that you will have to emulate before you are able to carry on the good work.

A lot of good agencies also keep track of the advertising done by their clients' main competitors. That too is worth digging out, provided you are careful not to be daunted by the mass of ideas that have already been tried. For every campaign theme that's ever seen the light of day, there are two more waiting to be born. And if you are wondering if any of them are ever going to strike you, you've come to the right place, because that's mostly what this book is about.

Finally, a word about your fellow copywriters. Naturally, they'll want to meet you, and they'll ask you what accounts you have been given to try your skills on. Mostly, this can be a pleasant and useful interchange of views, but on one point you should be careful: Do try not to pick up any of your compatriots' preconceived views. There's nothing worse than, when someone hears you are working on Brand X, to be told: "Oh you poor guy, that's a terrible account. They never buy anything good." Properly translated, that means: "I'm glad I got rid of that account, because I never did anything good on it."

don't knock it if you haven't tried it

I have known accounts that had such terrible reputations that it was very hard persuading any creative person in the agency to work on them. Then one day, a new guy arrives, and they pass this so-called terrible account on to him. Soon people begin to notice that this account is getting better and that the client is beginning to accept good work. And it isn't too long before it becomes a coveted account with quite a few people willing to work on it. What happened was that the new guy who joined knew that there were no such things as terrible accounts; there are simply terrible people working on them. I once got my hands on a single account worth over two and a half million dollars—the largest appropriation I have ever handled in my life. My mouth watered as I imagined the ads that kind of money made possible. After my third campaign hadn't got past the account controller's office, I still swore that it wasn't a terrible account. It was simply terribly handled. The client was being defrauded of value for money, had been badly advised and badly served for years, and when attempts were made to break that vicious cycle, they were stamped on because the account people "knew what the client wanted." Situations like this always end the same sad way. One day the account switches to a new agency that has prepared *a revolutionary new campaign,* and even as the first new ad appears you can hear the account people who lost the business saying: "But that's not what they want." Happily, the great majority of account people are only too pleased if they get some fresh thinking on the account, provided only that it is apposite. So be careful how your attitude towards your new place is colored. If you can put on your coat at going-home time, sure in the knowledge that you haven't picked up even the faintest whiff of disappointment about any of the accounts you have been asked to look after, believe me, you've done a good day's work.

The Creative Director

The chair behind the desk in the creative director's office is reckoned by many to be the hot-seat of the agency. Creative directors leave agencies more often than managing directors, financial directors, media directors, or even common or garden variety account directors who have seats on the board. Which is strange when you think how many of these there are, compared with the number of creative directors. Why should this be so? Is it that creative people are more temperamental, or more unstable, or have more itchy feet than the others? Is it that there are so few good creative directors that they are constantly being offered higher-paid, more enticing jobs? Or is it that the creative director's job *is* the hardest job in the agency?

You will find agency people who subscribe to all these reasons. I have a simpler explanation. The creative director is the one man in the agency whose job it is *easy to assess.* If the agency often produces outstanding creative work, wins new accounts, and retains its clients for long spells, then it can be safely assumed that the creative director is doing what is expected of him. If, on the other hand, the creative work is average to indifferent, if the agency has difficulty pulling in new accounts, and if clients complain more and more about the service they get, the place where it is easiest to *see* defects is simply by opening the nearest proof book. The work that comes out of the creative department is there for all to criticize if they wish (and when the chips are down, you'll find no shortage of critics).

creative work is there to be seen

An account man records the decisions that have been agreed on at meetings in his contact reports. A media man records his decisions in media schedules. A production man has to answer when an ad reproduces less than prettily. But who reads call reports a couple of weeks after they're written? Who digs out old media schedules and scans them to see if the buying was as efficient as it might have been? The production man picks up the phone, blasts the printer, and maybe gets a free insertion. But the creative work is all over the walls of the agency. The whole staff see it every day, and so does every visiting or prospective client. I have actually heard people in new briefings, referring to work done previously, say, "I hate that campaign!" Even clients, when they become dissatisfied, are likely to take it out on the creative work first. Research done by an agency I once worked for decreed that clients move in and out of agencies principally because of the caliber of the creative work. The ads themselves are all the general public ever sees. They are the only visible part of the agency's product. And although that product should include adventurous marketing thinking, genuinely entrepreneurial business advice, and exceptionally clever media buying, few people are in a position to judge whether all, or any, of that has been forthcoming. Yet everyone, down to the mail clerk, can tell you whether the ads are any good. When trouble looms, people look for it in the nearest place, and the nearest place is where they can see it on paper and film. And if the verdict is thumbs down, then it's the creative director who is frequently under that thumb.

By now I can hear the violins playing, the tears of mock sympathy flowing, and people saying, "If you don't like the heat, get out the kitchen." Believe me, I'm not complaining; I simply want to point out that there are times when the creative director is only as good as the last ad to come out of his department, whereas the account people are seldom judged on the contents of their last document. The creative director's job *is* the hardest job in the agency. Because although account people should primarily be shrewd businessmen with pleasing personalities, and creative people in the lower levels needn't have pleasant personalities as long as they produce the goods, a creative director has got to be able to write better ads than the rest of his department, be as good a business thinker as some of the best account people, have a pleasant way when he meets agency staff and clients, and be a very capable presenter. The qualifications needed for the job are pretty stiff, and there are not many people who can provide them; so creative directors get very good salaries, are very much in demand, and are more easily found out if they're not up to the mark.

don't tell me, show me

Let us consider in more detail the job of the creative director, since the lowliest creative person reading this book should, if he has any drive, eventually aspire to the job. The first requirement is that he should be able to create. The ads he makes should be the best in the agency, and the rest of his department should acknowledge they are best.

He may not make them very often, but he should be there as a backup, so when everything else fails and the agency has to find a creative solution to a problem, he can sit down with one colleague and make a campaign that fully does the job. And not *just* does the job, but does it in a way that takes creative work to its limits in terms of originality and ingenuity, but still with a totally sound business strategy behind it. And he should only be satisfied if the rest of his department then think to themselves: "I wish I'd done that."

Having produced that great work, and having done so in not too long a time (no client should expect to wait months for his campaign), then the creative director has to present that work. To do this he hasn't just got to be articulate with a pen in his hand. He must be able to talk clearly and concisely and think on his feet in front of a group of people who all the time are summing up his performance. What he is saying to a client, in essence, is, this is how the agency believes you should spend your next million dollars; and not only that, but if it was my own money, then this is how I would spent it myself. The techniques of presenting creative work have to be learned, and to that end I have given them a separate chapter in this book. But the very fact that I can write for a whole chapter about them should give you some idea of how complex the subject can be. Yet the best creative directors master this subject along with all the others they need at their fingertips, since there can be times when a campaign (or indeed a new account) is in the balance and when that balance is tipped by a highly professional presentation. It is interesting to note that when a panel of 60 clients was asked whom they would most expect to meet at a new business presentation, without exception they included the creative director. And you don't imagine for a moment that they wouldn't very quickly sum up his abilities as a presenter. If an agency is in a new business race, they are up against some of the smoothest, slickest, and most impressive talkers in town. Woe betide the man who shuffles, stammers, and loses the knife-like precision that lets you build a soundly reasoned argument.

all that, and more

We have agreed that the creative director should be able to make the best ads and then sell them. What other attributes does he need? Obviously, he should be an efficient administrator. He should control the flow of work through the agency, allocating accounts according to the abilities of the people under him. Some will be better at television; some will be better at good, sound, rational argument; some will have more skill with emotional claims. The creative director must be certain every account has a creative "mother and father." Somebody in his department must be directly responsible for the work of each client. He must get along with the client and be allowed as much contact with him as is sensible. As long as a creative person knows he is the *parent* of an account, you will have no trouble getting work done, and the work will generally be the best that person can produce. It's when the account has no creative parents that trouble starts. Nobody feels responsible for it, nobody wants to do it, standards quickly fall off, and the account comes to be known as a "bad" account. And as I have already emphasized, there are no such things as good or bad accounts; it's just that good or bad things have been done to them.

A creative director must be able to keep discipline. I don't mean by that that he should make the department clock in every morning, note the times they go to lunch (and the state in which they come back), and record those days when someone knocks off half-an-hour before quitting time. Sensible time-keeping is necessary, of course, but some of the best creative departments in the world are often empty at the peak hours of the working day. Discipline means that work is done when it is needed. And that doesn't mean five minutes before the internal review board, it means in sufficient time for revisions to be made if it is not up to standard. Discipline means that creative standards are maintained and that clients get the highest caliber of creative thinking the agency can produce. And not just the giants who spend three quarters of a million dollars or so each season, but the small companies who have a hundred and fifty thousand hard-earned dollars they can afford to put into an advertising appropriation and hope to get a campaign that has an effect out of all proportion to the money they spend. Here it is important that the creative director can set the example: Nothing is harder to do than ask a creative person to produce work he knows you can't produce yourself.

know who's who and what's what

Then our man must give credit where credit is due. Reva Korda has a phrase: "Who steals my credit steals cash." And it is true, for a good idea can win a creative person a raise in salary or even another job. I don't mean that the creative director must seek to know the origin of every slogan that ever comes before him and that he must search out the originator of every idea he sees. But sooner or later the people responsible for good work are recognized within the creative department itself, and the director must be sensitive enough to know when to say, "Well done," and to whom to say it, and sooner or later to discover who is pulling his weight and who is riding on the backs of his colleagues.

Another job the creative director has is to staff his department. It is difficult to tell in one interview, or even several interviews, whether the man or woman you are seeing will fit the job you have to offer. It is often hard to be sure whether he has even been responsible for all the work he is showing. There has been more than one occasion when I have been shown the same campaign by more than one creative team, each claiming responsibility for its conception. One managing director I spoke to reckoned his creative director was doing a fine job if only 50 percent of the men he hired were any good. In this respect, I acknowledge that the creative director has an easier job than a managing director, because at least the creative person has a portfolio of work and a reel of commercials by which he can be judged, whereas account and media people can only quote the accounts they have worked on, and who is to tell whether they worked on them well or not?

The creative director needs an ear to the business grapevine so he picks up information about who around town is making the good ads. One creative director I know used to scan the papers and watch TV avidly; and when he saw work that impressed him, he found out who did it; what agency they worked at; how much they were earning; and, lastly, whether or not they were interested in moving. And on more than one occasion, he phoned them himself to ask if they wanted to talk.

the king is dead, long live the king

A creative director should be concerned about his successor. When he sees a creative team steaming down the corridor with an armful of new concepts, on the way to present them to a client, he must be more pleased that they got along well and are gaining the confidence of their colleagues than suspicious whether they may be undermining his own position. He must encourage the people under him to take responsibility; think along the business lines he thinks along; produce work he would be happy to produce; and make decisions on those days when he is sick, or on vacation, or not around for a host of other reasons. He must appoint an assistant who, in an ideal world, is just as good as he is. He must have, besides the assistant, a team in which he has the utmost confidence. For even in the best-organized societies, creative directors can get run over by buses or be offered more attractive jobs at more ridiculous salaries. And it is then a creative director's responsibility to say: "John and Jean Smith are just as good at my job as I am, and when I go you can appoint them in my place with the utmost confidence. The standard of work will remain as high as it has been under my leadership, and all the things you have asked me to do I know they can do. So goodbye and thank you. You may rest in confidence that I have not left you in the lurch."

the grapevine

Those are the major functions of the creative director. He also has to do a hundred and one smaller things that no one writes into his job specifications, but which are vital if everything is to run smoothly. He must cut off nasty rumors that can arise even in the most smoothly running agencies. And to do that he must have an ear very close to the ground. Or, as commonly happens, he must have a discrete and loyal secretary who has an ear very close to the ground.

He must maintain a good relationship with the creative headhunters who proliferate our business, knowing when to phone them and being able to make a shrewd guess when other people in his department are phoning them. He should have good friends amongst other creative directors in town, for they can very often tell him about people he has interviewed and maybe would like to hire. He must take on the unenviable task of firing and do it justly but delicately. He must be able to say "no" to work without destroying the incentive of the people who did it and, instead, send them away burning with the will to do better next time. He must be able to disseminate ideas so that the people to whom he suggests them accept them in the right spirit and go away to interpret them without feeling that they will be deprived of their recognition when presenting the finished work.

which business is the creative director's business?

He must also make up his mind about what, in my experience, is the most difficult decision of all: just how much of the work he is going to do himself. There is a temptation, especially among the creative directors of small- and medium-sized agencies, to take the cream of the accounts— the public service campaigns and double-page spreads in the Sunday supplements—and make them himself, or with a favorite art director (for you will find that the great majority of creative directors began their careers as copywriters). In one sense this can be good, for it should mean that the prestige work the agency produces is of the highest caliber and will attract clients from outside who are looking for a change of agency. But in another sense this kind of behavior can be very bad because it destroys initiative. The people in the lower echelons of the department begin to feel they can stop trying, because the boss is going to work on the job too, and since he makes the decision about which of the ads should run, there is a hundred-to-one chance that he will recommend his own. I resolved the problem very simply. I let the existing accounts in the agency go on as smoothly as they might, and I put my back into new business presentations. For two reasons: One, because I believe every agency owes it to its existing clients to give them first priority as far as work is concerned, and really good work comes from the creative people who understand the account and know what the client expects from them. The second reason is that since, as creative director, I know I was expected to be in on all new business meetings and therefore should make the creative presentation myself, it ought to be my responsibility to do the work. A creative team, however conscientious, can sometimes be tempted to do less than their best if they know they are not going to be at the meeting to take the flak if anything goes wrong. I wanted to be sure, when prospective clients threw bricks, that they would throw them at me. Also, placed in a position of defending work, I would defend it wholeheartedly because it was *my* work. Naturally, I couldn't do all the new business pitches, and then the teams who made the ads made the presentation. This is important because it allows the prospect to meet the people who will actually work on his account. I also tried not to be there during those presentations but, instead, met the prospect afterwards, over a drink, when he was relaxed and seeking to get to know personalities in the agency.

watch the trap

I do *not* believe the myth that any one man can turn a so-called "non-creative" agency into a "creative" agency; indeed, I don't believe it has ever been done (although I have seen a number of highly creative agencies end up after a number of years producing very mediocre work). And I would advise creative people that if any agency offers you a creative director's chair on the premise, "Make us a creative shop," he should turn it down. The existing clients don't want a creative shop, and the existing agency hierarchy doesn't want a creative shop. Believe me, any account person who does want to work for a more creative agency should not have a great deal of difficulty moving into one.

If I have made the creative director's job seem difficult, then that is because it *is* difficult. If I have made it seem impossible, let me correct the impression, since there are a good many creative directors today doing a very good job. The post is demanding, even challenging, and every creative person worth his salt should grab the opportunity to take it if it is ever offered. For as a colleague of mine (also a creative director) once so appositely said: "It's the most fun you can have with your clothes on."

Good Habits
to Get Into

When I was a creative director, I used to make a point, once a day, of "doing the rounds"—that is calling on the people in my department and spending a few minutes talking with them. There were several reasons for this. First, I could see who was busy, what they were working on, and how the ads were progressing. If the people in one office weren't busy, then I could ask them about the workload, about what ads were going through the system, and whether they would favor taking on another job, or whether it was just one of the natural lulls that happen in the best-run businesses. It was also an opportunity to check up in case any group had too much work and to see if they could use a little help so everything would be done on time. And, naturally, I was there to pick up the complaints; such-and-such an ad hadn't been accepted, such-and-such an account person was proving difficult over a certain point; somebody wanted advice on which director to use to make a TV commercial; somebody else just wasn't happy that day. At the same time as smoothing things over, I could pass on any good news. Perhaps the agency was in the offing for a new account; perhaps one of the other groups had held a very good meeting with a client.

worry is the root of all evil

But sometimes, when I visited a team, they would be wrapped in thought; worse, they might be surrounded by a haze of anxiety because they were being pressed by copy dates to find a solution to a certain problem, and they hadn't a clue where it was going to come from. Ninety-nine times out of a hundred, this was simply because they hadn't prepared themselves properly for the job. It has got to be understood that effective, hard-working advertisements do not arrive out of thin air. Copywriting is not a case of saying simply, "OK, guys, let's think of a good idea." Picking thoughts from the wide blue yonder and attaching them to products may be what the student or trainee thinks a creative person's job is. I have even found some account people—and not inexperienced ones either—who believe that is how things are done.

begin at the start

It is nothing of the sort. Over the years, I have learned there is a lot to do before you finally settle down to make an ad. You should be quite clear about the size of the advertisement required: page, single-column ad, giant bill-board, two-minute film, or whatever. If you are doing a press ad, then you should rule out the type area on your layout pad so you can see quite clearly how many square inches you have to fill. Once you can *see* that space, get copies of the magazine or newspaper in which the ad is to appear. Either find some back numbers from your library or, if they have none, go out to the stands and buy the current issue.

Read that magazine. Check the editorial for matters of interest; get a sense of the style; see how technical the writing is; note the kind of illustrations used, how they are captioned, and whether there is a predominance of photographs or line drawings. Check on the quality of the paper, find out how the publication is printed (this will guide you as to how big photographic illustrations must be to reproduce clearly), and make a note in your head of any special techniques the editor is using to increase readership. Then turn to the employment pages: this will show you what kind of people read the magazine, what kind of jobs they do, what qualifications they have, and how much money they earn. You see, already you are getting to know quite a bit about the audience you will be talking to. You can decide how technical your own writing must be and whether to be subtle or straightforward in your approach.

Next, find out on what date your advertisement will appear and whether that date has any special significance. It might be an anniversary for a certain manufacturer; it might be on a day when the publication is running a special supplement, or a day when a trade show is about to be opened.

Look at the ad requisition to see if you are given color or black and white to work in. If black and white, will color (maybe just "spot" color—a single second color) help to get your message over any better, and if so, how much extra will it cost? Where in the publication is your ad to run: inside the front cover, next to the contents page, next to the editorial, next to the employment ads, inside the back cover, outside the back cover, or run-of-paper (that is, wherever the make-up man on the publication feels like putting it).

bleeding in the gutter

If you have a double-page spread, see whether you have the center of the magazine to work with; then you don't have to worry about things like where your headline splits or whether part of your picture will disappear in the gutter (the fold where the publication is stitched). Ask whether your ad will bleed—that is, be trimmed flush to the edge of the page (this is normally about 10 percent extra) or whether you are working to a type area, in which case your ad will have a white border around it. If you haven't got bleed, you might want to try to get it, since it will let you say more—I mean in terms of the forcefulness of your communication rather than in terms of content. Bleed doesn't mean you should use more words.

Finally, check whether the publication has a correspondence section. This will give you an insight into what readers think, how literate they are, and what particular matters are currently on their minds. It may be that you can incorporate a particular subject into your ad (provided the insertion date is not so far ahead that readers will have forgotten the correspondence). A glance at the leader—most magazines have one—can also help. And keep an eye peeled on views that appear to be unpopular; it's worth knowing what not to say as well as what people want to hear.

All right, the first part of your preparation is over. And you see how helpful it has been. Yet when I did my rounds I frequently found cases where the creative group not only didn't have a copy of the magazine their ad was to run in, but they'd never even heard of it.

So you have the publication, you have drawn up the space in that publication you want to fill, and you know when the ad is to run. Now, turn to the product.

you cannot find out too much about your product

If it is small enough to get onto your desk, put it there. If it's too big for that, get as many photographs of it as you can. And start to study. If you are writing a campaign for the product for the first time, and if you have plenty of time, don't be afraid to ask for a tour of the factory. Few things can help you understand your client and get the inside facts on how his goods are made better than a tour of his business. Let me give you an example. I was once asked to write a campaign for Church Shoes, probably the best-known and most expensive shoes made in England. They cost more wholesale than a great many shoes from other makers cost retail. So you see, we had a price problem. I wanted to find out where all the money was going.

I spent a day watching the shoes being made. The soles were stamped out of 2-inch-thick leather. They were stitched to the uppers with thread that was waxed by hand. The shoes were actually made in *pairs*: there was none of the business of making half a million left shoes, the same number of right shoes, and pairing them off at the end of the line. It took over 200 different operations to make a single shoe; each was polished by hand with camel-hair brushes to give a scratch-free shine; and the final embossing, with the size, style, and brand name, was done in 22-carat gold. I came away convinced that although the shoes were very expensive, they were worth every penny.

I wouldn't have discovered any of this if I hadn't asked to tour the factory; and when the ad was written and presented to Church's managing director, even he didn't know everything about his shoes that my advertisement told him.

information sells

And that is the next secret of making good ads. *Tell the reader something he doesn't know.* Now obviously you're not going to be able to do that if you simply write from your own general knowledge. So if you are going to advertise a car, you have first got to drive it; a food, and you have first got to eat it; a refrigerator, and you've got to go to a showroom and persuade a salesperson to "sell" it to you, while you compare it with the competition you are up against; a service—say car rental—and you have got to experience it; a job, and you've got to speak to the people who do it, find why they enjoy it, and how they got into it in the first place. First-hand experience of whatever you have to sell makes for first-rate ads. If you haven't got the straw, you can't make the bricks to build a sales argument. Once you've steeped yourself in the product and heard the story from the maker's point of view, find out what other people think about it. If you're selling a car, read the car news; if you're selling a detergent, speak to the housewife; a beauty product, speak to the woman who uses it and find out why, and what it does for her. An independent, unbiased opinion is worth half-a-dozen claims from the maker, and that opinion is even more valuable if it comes from someone well qualified to comment. And don't forget the proof book. You may well discover, buried in the body text of an old ad, a fact with which to build a new headline. Now let me give you an example of how someone uncommitted to a brand can still help you sell it.

what about the workers?

I was asked to make an ad for a stove. I went to see it being built and to the retailers to see how well it stood up surrounded by other stoves. Then I found a steel technician who hadn't made a stove in his life but understood all about the gauge and quality of metals. I looked up an electrician who'd never wired a stove but knew good work when he saw it. I spoke to an enameller who had worked on baths but not stoves, and finally I talked to an insulation expert (again, he had nothing to do with stoves but understood the insulation principles involved). All of them, when they saw the stove for the first time, agreed it was good. Hence the ad was headlined: A testimonial for Brand X stoves from four people who've never used one in their lives.

There is another reason why you should be completely *au fait* with your product. Not only will you make good ads, but you will be in an excellent position to explain and defend your work. An account person can destroy your ad if he comes up with a fact that you know nothing about. Not only will you look a fool, you will have proved to him that you simply haven't done your homework. On the other hand, few things impress a client more than the creative person who demonstrates he knows as much about the product as the man who actually manufactures it. Demonstrating that you have researched it, checked up on how the public see it, and dug out information for yourself immediately increases the client's confidence in you and dismisses any suspicion that you are working from ignorance. He warms to your professionalism and is more inclined to accept your recommendations.

So now you know a lot about the magazine your ad is to appear in, a little about the people who read the magazine, and, hopefully, everything there is to know about the product you are selling. Now you have to find out about the people you are selling to. *Who is the customer?* To find out about the market, you can first go through all the documents likely to be in the agency. What age is the prospect? What does he earn? Where does he live? Where and how does he buy? In short, *who are you talking to?* I am going to say a lot more about what we call, in advertising jargon, "the target audience" in Chapter 4, but you will get a tremendous amount of help when you get down to making your ad if you can "see" that audience in your mind's eye.

you're part of a team, good buddy

Finally, you settle down to work. Be sure to remember, as I said in Chapter 1, to work *with* your art director. I once knew a writer who came into the agency early, before his art director arrived, sat at his typewriter, and freewheeled for an hour, hoping an idea would come to life. This, in my view, is quite the wrong way to work. Until you have thought of the concept, until you have reached the main idea, you should work on your layout pad. You might find it helps to actually write headlines into the exact space that you have to fill (remember I said to draw that out first). But before you write anything, talk. Decide what your main thought should be; use your colleagues' brains, because two heads can produce more together than each can produce separately. And remember, although you are the writer, there is no reason why your art director can't come up with a headline, or, for that matter, why you can't have the idea for the picture. Get the feel of the person you are working with and work as a team. I once knew a young copywriter who couldn't bear his art director to write headlines. No matter how good a headline appeared, if it came from the artist, this particular young man would say, "Yes, very good," then pause for a moment and try to paraphrase the same thought. I'm not knocking persistence or the attempt to refine and express in fewer, better words a partcular product claim; I'm knocking the inability to acknowledge that an art director can think of the right words. The problem arose from a feeling of insecurity and a need for that writer to constantly prove himself. Happily, as he gained experience and got closer to his art man, he relaxed, and the two became a very good team. Later, they left that particular agency for a nice, fat salary elsewhere. Of course, the problem can apply in reverse to art directors, so if either of you find yourselves doing it to the other, stop.

A great idea, as David Bernstein says in his book, *Creative Advertising* (Longmans), doesn't care who has it. And what matters is not who has it, but whether the other guy is big enough to recognize it. Or brave enough to say, "That's garbage," when a second-rate idea appears. Some of the art directors I've worked with were valuable because they could *discriminate*—the good from the bad, the better from the good—and they could put their finger on the best idea no matter where it came from (even from a media or account person).

"I" didn't do it, "we" did it

Present your work as a team. When you agree what you are going to do, do it with a united front. You don't have to make it plain to the creative director that it was your idea or that it was Charlie's idea; if he's a good creative director, he'll assume you worked together and will not need to know where the initial spark came from. Sooner or later the true source of an idea makes itself felt: Like murder, it speaks with most miraculous organ.

There is another aspect of this relationship with your art director. There will be times when your colleague simply can't have an idea. This might go on for a time; try as he may, nothing he suggests comes up to his usual standard, and you find the onus of the work falling on you. Whatever you do, don't criticize him. For two reasons. One, because silent criticism doesn't just hurt the person it is directed at—*it inhibits him from returning to good form.* And two, if you silently nail him when he has a barren spell, then you'll be nailed yourself when you have one, and nothing is more destructive for either of you. This is not to say you should forever carry a deadweight. This is a waste of time and, eventually, if you keep providing the solutions, the other guy stops thinking for himself; his advertising brain seizes up.

I have worked with most types of art directors, and one thing is sure: The system that used to prevail in the old days of the copywriter sitting in one room writing the words and the clerk carrying them to another room where the art director added a picture was a waste of the talent of both men. When we come to how ads are made in more detail, I hope you will understand that the picture and the headline should work in conjunction with each other and that there can be times when neither makes sense on its own. More often than not, when that happens, you have made a very good ad, and it could never happen if the two men in the team didn't speak to each other.

a line and an outline

The method of working should be simple. You both kick around ideas for as long as you need to and then maybe put down two or three on a layout pad. They should consist only of a sketch of the illustration and a headline, and the message of the ad should come across as though you are making a poster. As you turn out the first draft ideas, pin them on your wall. Some groups like to give their ads what they call "the overnight test"; that is, they make no decision about them until the next day, when they can come into the office fresh and see if what seemed quite brilliant yesterday still has the same impact 24 hours later. If it doesn't, you should have no compunction about scrapping it. I once saw a "house" ad for a particular agency that claimed that most places would present to their clients work this agency threw away—an indication of how long they persevered in their search for an outstanding idea.

When you are doing very small ads (by which I mean 2-, 4-, or 6-inch single or double columns), it can help to work *in that size space* on your layout pad. That way, you get a true idea of how big the headline is going to appear, and it's easy to tell how many words you can sensibly include. It may seem hard to start with, but since you have to take a long time to get things right (both looking right and reading right), you pay much more attention to economy in words and speed of communication. You may not work like that later in your job-life, but when you are gaining experience and can't tell by instinct when your copy is overlength, it is a good habit to cultivate. The habit of drawing up the type area can help whatever size of ad you are doing. It can show you whether you need all the space to tell the story or, conversely, whether you can't possibly tell the story in so small a space. Don't work directly on your typewriter before you have a format worked out. The time to start tapping the keys is when you get down to making the body copy, and a good rule to remember here is that you should never use two words when one will do.

poetry don't sell

Many copywriters, when they start off, take a great deal of time developing a style. What is much more important is that you get the *content* of the ad right. Alliteration, flowing phrases, puns, and pretty turns of phrase may have their place, but it is way behind making sense of what you are saying and communicating the message simply, clearly, and concisely.

I once had a man come to me for an opinion on a piece of copy. I read it a couple of times, then sat down, and together we condensed it into a third of its length without leaving out a single piece of relevant information. I thought the man would have been well pleased, but when I saw the ad typeset a few days later, it was back to its original length. And when I asked him about it, he said he wanted to preserve his style. This is sheer self-indulgence, since the best style to have is the most economic style. Readers don't have time (nor any inclination) to admire the style in which ads are composed. They want to know "what's in it for me?" So use short words, pithy words, and be as brief as you can without missing out any point that will help make the sale. Remember, though you may aspire to being a poet, while you are being paid by a client, you are a salesman—and a very business-like one too. Interesting copy is copy that moves at a pace, gives a real reward for reading, and keeps telling you things you don't know and yet can easily believe. There is a great deal of value in a piece of advertising copy that *astonishes*, always provided that it rings true.

so, to summarize

First, use the tools at your command: pen and layout pad. Get down the size of the ad you have to make. Then get the publication in which it is to appear. Then find out everything you can about the product (if possible, keep it on your desk). Then find out all you can about the person you want to sell it to. Then start thinking. Talk over your thoughts with your art director and put two or three of them down on paper. Pin the paper to your wall and give it "the overnight test." Be ruthless with anything that is less than excellent. Economize with your words. Try to create telegrams—that is, pictures and headlines that telegram the message. Make allowances for each other, and recognize that neither of you has a monopoly on the words or the pictures. In the end, together, you should have made one good ad, which, as they say, is what it's all about.

There Are
Only Two Kinds
of Advertising

There are:

Newspaper and magazine ads	Classified ads
Television ads	Corporate ads
Direct mail ads	Legal ads
Mail order ads	Book and record club ads
Retail ads	Health insurance ads
Financial ads	Posters
Employment ads	

And you can probably think of more. So what do I mean when I say there are only two kinds of ads? Simple; whatever kind of ad you pick from the above list, it must fall into one of two categories:

1. Ads where there is something to say.

2. Ads where there is nothing to say.

Let us deal with the obvious objection to that paragraph, which is, as any experienced creative person will tell you, that every ad should have something to say. Very true. And it is the creative person's job to make sure every ad says something. But there are many occasions when there is little or nothing of substance to say. For example, you are asked to make a commercial for a tin of beans. Now what can you tell the million or so housewives who buy them every day about a tin of beans? Isn't anything you say about them likely to be such common knowledge that your commercial ends up being utterly banal? There is, in fact, virtually nothing you can tell a woman about baked beans that *(a)* will interest her and *(b)* she doesn't already know. That's what I mean by the kind of advertising where the creative person has nothing to say.

But first let us look at the area where there is something to say. Happily, there are a great number of products that carry good stories and allow creative people to devise factual claims and produce informative advertising. To name a few, I would say ads for cars, washing machines, stereos, insurance, vacations, and any kind of entertainment—all have plenty to say. And in those cases (and obviously I have only listed a minute fraction of them), the important thing is—*say it.*

first silver rule

That is the first principle in making good ads: *When you have something to say, say it.* But having made such a positive statement, I want to make a further point. You may have a product about which there is a great deal to

WE IMPROVED THE BEST MILEAGE CAR IN AMERICA.

Where do you go from up?

In the case of the 1981 Volkswagen Rabbit Diesel, we went under the hood.

We made the engine larger than it was, and added enough extra horsepower to zip you from 0 to 50 in 11.4 brief seconds.

And that was just for starters.

On the outside, we gave the Rabbit Diesel a handsome new grille.

More visible directional signals in front.

And more visible taillights in back.

Inside, there's a whole new interior.

With a sleek new instrument panel; plusher, more comfortable seats; and an improved heating and air conditioning system that can get you up or down to 68° faster than ever.

Altogether, we made close to 1,000 changes, refinements and improvements in the Rabbit Diesel for 1981.

But for all of those, the most impressive thing about it is the one thing we didn't change.

And that's its fuel economy.

The Rabbit Diesel still gets better mileage than every other car in the country.

In fact, the four-speed Rabbit Diesel gets even better mileage than it did last year.

For the four-speed, EPA estimated 42 mpg, 56 mpg highway estimate. (Use "estimated mpg" for comparison to other cars. Mpg varies with speed, trip length and weather. Actual highway mpg will probably be less.)

If you're thinking about a diesel, you really should look at this one.

There isn't another diesel on the road that comes close to it.

But then, we started with a big advantage when we built the 1981 Rabbit Diesel.

We started with the 1980.

VOLKSWAGEN DOES IT AGAIN

© 1980 VOLKSWAGEN OF AMERICA

say. In that case, you must simplify your story, so you spearhead your ad, whether it be a print ad or a commercial, with a single thought. It should be the essence of the claim you want to make, the one aspect of the product you most want people to remember. You will make very little headway if you try to produce work that has a great many ideas bursting out of it; in a 30-second TV commercial, your audience will not be able to remember more than one thought. When you make a print ad, your headline and picture are unlikely to be able to communicate more than one thought. And in the cases where you have a complex story to tell, you may need to spend a lot of time discussing with the client, the account people, and your creative partner what the one thought should be.

Let me quote an example. A tire manufacturer I once worked with invented a new tire. It was a radial tire. It had a completely new tread design. Under the rubber was a nylon strip that reduced wear. Underneath the nylon strip was a steel belt that pushed the tire down firmly on the road and greatly increased grip in wet weather. And the tire was being offered at a very competitive price. You can see at once that there is a great deal to say about such a product, but what is most important is that any advertising communicates one major thought. The supporting sales points can be mentioned, of course, but one big idea should come out of any campaign devised for that tire. The thought we finally chose was SAFETY—that this new tire increased the safety of motorists, whatever the weather conditions. The commercials concentrated on situations where a driver needed his tire to grip the road. We featured a windshield shattering on a highway, where the car came to a swift, safe halt; an intersection where a cyclist swerved in front of the car, which was able to stop in time; and a demonstration of some tailor's dummies falling in front of the car, which was able to avoid crushing them (the parallel with real people is obvious). The point I want to emphasize is that all the ads were single-minded. They had something to say—that the tire made driving safer—and they said it simply, yet very dramatically, time and again. There was no question of dissipating the advertising effort by making one film about the steel, one about the nylon, one about the low price, and so on. So to summarize so far, if you have something to say, say it. Say it simply, say it dramatically, and be completely single-minded about your claim. To quote an old advertising adage, repetition is reputation.

the unique proposition

One advertising man took this principle to a very firm conclusion. Mr. Rosser Reeves, who was first a copywriter, then creative director, and finally a senior partner in a leading American agency, developed what he

FRESH KILLED CHICKEN

When the product you're selling is similar to everyone else's—in similar grades, from similar pumps, on similar routes for similar prices—how do you *fascinate* the customer? This Mobil campaign is one of the best-ever examples of the maxim: "When there's nothing to say, use showmanship." (Art director: *Len Sirowitz*)

Fresh-killed chicken.

Bravo.

Let's hear it for the winner

That's him lying there – the dead one.

Or is he the loser?

You can't tell. Not that it matters very much. Because in the idiot game of "chicken," winners and losers both die.

In the idiot game of "chicken," two cars speed straight for each other. Head on.

With luck, one car steers clear in the nick of time.

Without luck, neither car steers clear. And the winner and the loser are equally dead.

Some "game."

It took God Almighty to stop Abraham from making a blood sacrifice of his son.

What do you suppose it will take to make us stop sacrificing *our* children?

We who bear them in sterilized hospitals, stuff them with vitamins, educate them expensively, and then hand over the keys to the car and wait with our hearts in our mouths.

Too bad we educate them only to make a living and not to stay alive.

Because right now – this year – car accidents kill more young people than anything else. Including war. Including cancer. Including *anything*.

Yet we allow it.

Incredibly enough, fewer than half the young people who get drivers' licenses every year have passed a driver training course.

Which leaves well over 2 million (!) youngsters who get licenses every year *without* passing such a course.

And this is the price we pay: 13,200 young people between 15 and 24 died in automobile accidents in 1965. (The exact number for 1966 isn't in yet; it will probably be higher.)

It's a gruesome answer to the population explosion.

And if we all sit still about it, we ourselves are guilty of "chickening out."

Yet we mustn't frighten our youngsters; they're frightened enough.

We must teach them.

Does your school system have a driver training course?

Are there books in your school library or public library on driving? (Did you know such books exist? Do *they* know?)

Are the requirements for getting a driver's license in your state tough enough?

Are your radio and TV stations paying any attention to the problem? Your newspapers?

Does anyone in your community give awards for *good* driving? The PTA? Or the Boy Scouts? The Chamber of Commerce? The churches or synagogues?

What kind of driver are you yourself? Do you set a good example or a poor one?

Would your company insist on a driver training course before they'd hire someone?

Would your schools insist on a training course before they'd turn a youngster loose?

Would it help?

Yes, it would. Education works. Drivers in large truck fleets are trained to drive safely. And some of them have dropped accident rates to only about half that of the general public.

It would cost little or nothing to get these things going. And we haven't a minute to spare. It's blood that we have on our hands, not time.

We at Mobil sell gasoline and oil for our living *to* the living. Naturally, we'd like young people to grow up into customers. But for now we'd be happy if they'd simply grow up.

Mobil
We want you to live.

called the philosophy of the Unique Selling Proposition. This is abbreviated now to USP. Reeves' idea was simple; the agency had to go through the benefits of the product until they could find something unique to say about it.

Or, if there really was nothing unique, then they had to find a feature of the product that nobody else was using and make it their own. The unique feature was the Unique Selling Proposition and was meant to represent the one feature which that product, and only that product, could offer the consumer. Reeves attached this philosophy to the agency he worked at (Ted Bates and Co.), so it too had a USP. He helped to build it into one of America's largest and most successful shops. When Ted Bates bought their way into British advertising, they brought the USP philosophy with them, and it led to some very strange campaigns. When advertising a chocolate button with a sugar glazing, the USP they found was, "melts in your mouth, not in your hand." And for a boiled sugar candy, "double-wrapped to keep in the freshness." Never mind what the candy tasted like, or that candy makes kids happy so the commercials should be happy. Bates were determined to find USPs, even if they were so far down the line of customer requirements as to be virtually irrelevant. It took them some years, and the departure of not a few creative people, to accept that there were times when a product simply did not have a viable Unique Selling Proposition. But it is not my intention to knock the idea of USP; I use it to emphasize the importance of being single-minded in your advertising, looking for the main sales point, and then pushing it home in all the promotional material so you make a real impact.

second silver rule

So much for those times when the product offers you something to say. Now what about the times when you have nothing to say? I include in this product category beers, gasolines and oils, steam-baked breads, canned fruits, most cigarettes, butter, margarines, and most shampoos, deodorants, and hair sprays. Not only is there very rarely anything you can say about them the public doesn't already know, but they are also products which command the largest appropriations. They spend a great deal of money, they often use a great many changes of copy, and yet there is nothing to say. The principle here is quite simple: *When you have nothing to say, use showmanship.*

As usual, an example will help to clarify. I once wrote a campaign for the humble salted peanut, the kind you nibble in bars, give to kids at parties, and serve to friends who come over for drinks. There's not much to say about salted peanuts. Everyone's tried them at some time and it's hard not to like them. And although these particular nuts were popular there was nothing extraordinary about them; the brief boiled down to "make people love our nuts!" Well they won't love your nuts if they hate your commercials, so the obvious route to try was humor. We came to the thought that the nuts were so enjoyable that you felt like saying "aw shucks" when the last one was gone. And wrapped that up in the line: "The nuts you hate to come to the end of." Not exactly mind-blowing, so we had to devise an extraordinary film. It opened with King Kong tipping a giant bag of nuts down his throat and munching happily. But when he comes back for a second mouthful the pack is empty, whereupon he starts to tear New York apart.

When you've established the idea, the variations are endless. Our next film was about a high court judge, surreptitiously nibbling the nuts while trying a case. He eats the last one just as he's about to pass sentence, and the prisoner goes down for twenty years. Pure entertainment. We couldn't say the nuts were bigger or more popular or better roasted or more nutritious than anyone else's. They weren't even the top seller. So we used *showmanship*.

Another brief summary, so you have got the two most important principles about making ads fixed firmly into your mind. First, when you have something to say, say it. Second, when you have nothing to say, use showmanship. If you remember these principles, you will save yourself hours of heartache searching for stories to tell about products that have no stories to tell. At the same time, you will avoid foolish campaigns, where there is a real story but you bury it under a welter of borrowed interest.

don't seek where you won't find

In my early days as a copywriter, the idea that I might be presented with a product that had half a million dollars to spend, about which there would be virtually nothing to say, never occurred to me. And this "blindness" to the way campaigns were written led to some sleepless nights, as I turned over in my mind the problems of writing a campaign about, say, beer, which had a certain taste (but no very distinctive one), was brewed for a brief spell, and was then distributed. With those few meager facts, how could I ever produce an exciting advertising campaign? If only someone had pointed out to me that it was no use looking for an advertising campaign that talked exclusively about the product.

So how is it done? Let us consider a highly successful campaign for beer—the one for Heineken. Once it's pointed out, it is easy to see that the advertising is not about the beer *per se*, it's about the effect a beer might have if it could reach the parts of the body that beer cannot reach. I am in no way decrying the advertising (I consider it brilliant), but I am showing the would-be copywriter that if he directs his attention solely to the product, he may never find good creative solutions. The answer lies, as I have already said, in showmanship: Show policemen wriggling their toes as the beer revives them; show a potter using his skill again as the beer takes effect. It's highly imaginative stuff, and it captures the imagination of drinkers all over the country, but in no way is it about Heineken. It's an illogical extension of the effect good drink has on the psyche.

animal imagery

Another product I listed amongst those that have nothing to say is gasoline. Let us look at what was probably the most effective campaign of the 1960s: the job done for Esso—"Put a tiger in your tank." Figures show that this campaign persuaded more drivers to switch from their usual gas to Esso than any other gasoline campaign before or since. But is the campaign about the gasoline? Certainly not, it's about getting the power of a tiger into your engine; the decorations around the pump hose-pipes, the tiny tiger tails to affix to your driving mirror, and the majestic tigers leaping over billboards having nothing to do with the gasoline. All you can tell drivers about the real Esso is that it comes in a number of grades, that it is refined to suit any engine, and that you can pick it up anywhere in the country, all of which they know perfectly well already. You see, now that it is pointed out, that the ads didn't talk about Esso gasoline at all, and that if they had, they would have been very dull ads. But hit on a slogan such as "Put a tiger in your tank" and you have a theme you can develop for years. Forget the technical details; go for excitement, fun, and the ingeniousness of an idea. And offer those humorous little give-aways like tiger tails, and you'll have crowds lining up at the pumps.

There is another gasoline campaign that worked well at the pumps— the Shell Make Money campaign. This was a contest where you picked up half a fake dollar bill every time you bought gasoline, and if you were lucky, you got two halves that fitted together perfectly, which you could exchange for hard cash. The technique was eventually declared illegal, but that is not the point here; the point is that it wasn't about Shell gasoline— it was about collecting enough half bills to make money.

have gamez with beanz

Let us consider one final example. I started this chapter by telling you there was nothing to say about cans of baked beans; yet in the UK Heinz spends up to two million dollars a year advertising them, and they do it very effectively. But do they talk about the beans? Not directly, no. In one campaign, they show young children saying witty rhymes about where they had a snack and what they had to eat. The kids are the main attraction, and the fun in the rhymes makes us listen and grin. But they don't tell you how many beans are in the can, nor what the beans are (who knows what baked beans are?), nor how the delicious tomato sauce is made; the only fact you can gather from the Heinz baked beans advertising is that a million housewives open up a can every day. This in itself is impressive, and they add that brilliant slogan, "Beanz Meanz Heinz," at the end. The ads are not about beans; they are about the people who buy them and about the fun you can have if you play games with the letter z.

look beyond the product

Those examples should show the young copywriter that he has to look further than the product if he is going to develop a campaign the advertiser can put money behind. He can talk about who uses the product, where they use it, when and how they use it, or why they use it. These techniques I will deal with much more fully later in this book. I have spent so much time developing this theme to help you avoid the pitfalls I stumbled into in my career. I made a point in the last chapter of telling you to put the product on your desk before you started to write about it, but you could spend a year staring at a can of beans and not get a campaign out of it that was worth a row of beans. This is why it is vital that you go for facts; discover the story of the baked bean, where it comes from, how it's grown, who first imported it. Do anything to get information, because without it you will never get an idea. But in the last analysis, with products of this kind, it is showmanship that counts. And this is where the writer and art directors have to put on their caps and think. But even wild thinking is not enough unless you know the techniques you can use to help you devise campaigns. There are a lot of them, and as you progress in the business you will learn to recognize when a particular technique has been used. Chapters 6, 7, and 8 list many techniques you will find useful. If you are an ingenious writer, you may, as you gain experience, invent some of your own; and you can be sure, if you do, that the rest of the business will be hard on your heels, taking your idea and using it for themselves, with their own particular twist added to make it just that little bit different. There's nothing new under the sun, but there are certainly new ways of seeing and solving old problems, and that is part of our craft.

easy campaigns—and hard ones

I would like to end this chapter with a word about campaigns that strike you as brilliant; you must learn to judge whether they rest on the ingeniousness of the writer and art director *finding* something to say or whether the interest was actually in the product itself, and all they did (all?) was dig it out. You may have noticed some ads—for contraception, for road safety, and for moderation in drinking, for example—have received acclaim from advertising people, and rightly so. But it has to be said—and this is no denigration of the skill of the creative people involved—that contraception *is* a subject that arouses a great deal of interest, not to say controversy. And road safety allows creative people to show road accidents—and how they actually happen—which, in itself, is mighty interesting. And the very clever techniques of the anti-booze advertising campaigns, which invite you to find out for yourself whether you are on the path to alcoholism, are fascinating to read because they can ring a bell in our daily lives. Please let this be clear: I am not decrying the skills of the writers who made these campaigns; less talented people would have made a much worse job of them. I *am* saying that some subjects are intrinsically interesting, and I think you will find it easier to do good work on these subjects than you will on products that, of themselves, have little or nothing to make you sit up and think.

So, one final summary. Decide whether your product has anything to say; if it has, say it. If it hasn't, don't waste fruitless hours trying to dig out some obscure fact that you hope will give you a campaign. Use showmanship. Look well outside the product itself to the people, the times, the places, and the ways the product is used. Above all, be interesting. The next chapters will show you how.

Work on What to Say, Not on How to Say It

One of the hardest things to learn when you first begin to write copy is how *not* to do it. This is because the average Joe thinks the craft consists mainly of being clever with words. That's not what copywriting is about at all. Someone else said a copy person was an advocate for a client's product and that it was his job to make out the best possible case for it; I define it simply as "making someone want to do something." You make them want to own a particular car, or use a particular service, or wear particular clothes. And although you should be able to use words cleverly, it is much more important that you are *articulate* in print than that you can play the fool with grammar, spelling, or quotations. Throw away your *Thesaurus*, put down your books of *bon mots*, and jettison all that junk of half-remembered phrases from your poetry and English literature classes. None of that is going to help you, and the only reference book any copywriter really needs is a dictionary, and that only because he may need to correct his spelling.

There is another attitude of mind that inhibits people from making good ads, and that is the need to impress. This is very invidious, and I am not suggesting there's anything wrong with the writer wanting himself and his work to be well thought of. But you can end up in a situation where you sit down with your art director, and each says to the other: "This ad has got to be great!" And the very desire to make a "great" ad actually impedes you doing it, because you are starting at the wrong end.

There is nothing out of place with imposing high creative standards on your work; in fact, I believe the creative team should be its own toughest critic. But do not work to make impressive ads; work to sell the product or service, and you will impress if the ad does the job that it's intended to. The way to start work is to prepare yourself as I described in Chapter 3. You get your layout pad, your felt-tip pens, the paper your ad is going into, and the product (hopefully) on your desk. Then refer to "The Strategy."

the advertising strategy

An advertising strategy is prepared by the client, the account people, and the creative people, together. They examine all the aspects of the product, the market, distribution, profit target, and the appropriation backing the product; then they devise a plan of campaign. When the plan is agreed on, the agency sets it down in a document and sends it to the client. The client passes it around to the people in his company who want to know what direction the advertising is to take. Those people may make comments that the client will then relay back to the agency. If corrections are

IT HAS ECONOMY WRITTEN ALL OVER IT

There's a lot you can say about a good truck. But not all at once. So your advertising strategy has to single out your main selling thought. And when I say the bones of the advertising strategy stick out of this ad like a skeleton, I mean it only as a compliment. (Art director: *Bob Tucker*)

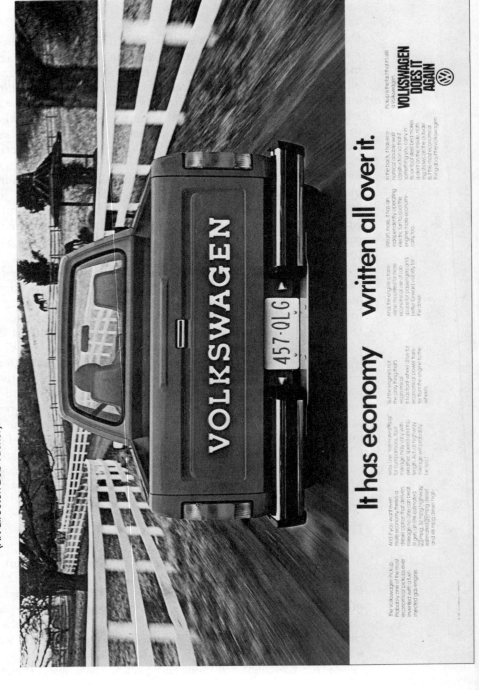

It has economy   written all over it.

The Volkswagen Pickup. Probably one of the most economical pickups ever invented, with a fuel-injected gas engine.

And if you want even more economy, there's a diesel option that gives you mileage no other pickup with a diesel engine can beat at gas or EPA estimated 32 mpg, 37 mpg highway estimated (39 mpg diesel and 46 mpg diesel highway).

way. Use "estimated mpg" for comparison. Your actual mileage may vary with weather, speed and trip length. Actual highway mileage will probably be less.)

But the engine's not the only thing that's economical.

It has both wheel drive for economical power transfer from the engine to the wheels.

And the engine has a front-wheel-mounted to make economical use of cab space for labor-saving and better forward visibility for the driver.

What's more, it has an independently operating electric fan to cool the engine more economically too.

In the back, that eco-nomical double-wall construction so that if something you carry in its overload sted bed makes a dent on the inside, both the inside and the outside. Put the most economical thing about the Volkswagen

Pickup is the fact that's still a Volkswagen.

VOLKSWAGEN DOES IT AGAIN

457-QLG

required, the agency will make them—the account and creative people working together again. The revised version is returned to the client, and he seeks agreement to it from the people at his end. Finally, it comes back to the agency signed and sealed, and the agency then sets out a plans document, which should be the bible on how the product is to be promoted.

A strategy will tell you:

Who the target is.

What offer you have to put to them.

What evidence you have to show the offer is worthwhile.

What final impression you want to leave.

That may not be the way the strategies read in your office, since every agency has its own method of putting down what the advertising should achieve, but that should be the gist of what they mean. Forms may differ, but the content should be the same. Let there be no mistake about how important a strategy is. Nor should anyone feel it is a device to restrict the creative person. A strategy is the result of hard thinking by everyone concerned with the product. Creative people should always be consulted before the strategy is drawn up, and any account person who dares to produce a strategy without consulting the creative department deserves all the flak he gets.

strategies help you sell your work

You, as a creative person, should be grateful for a strategy for a number of reasons. First, it points you in a direction and puts you under a discipline that can prevent hours of useless work. A strategy shouldn't tell you exactly what to do in your ad; it can be more helpful in telling you what *not* to do. Dozens of irrelevant ideas that you might have been tempted to develop can be discarded, thanks to the strategy. It saves you time, it saves you work, it stops you going up creative blind alleys. If you like, it's a map that tells you where the gold is buried and says, "Dig here." Another fact to remember is that strategies protect your work; they make it much more difficult for a client to reject a campaign for the wrong reasons. If your ads talk to the audience defined in the strategy, if each makes a promise as defined in the strategy and does it in an interesting and out-of-the-ordinary manner, then the work cannot easily be rejected. Irrational judgments, subjective views, whether or not the client likes the color of the model's dress, and so on, are of no weight when checking to see if a campaign is a true interpretation of a strategy.

And if the client's people believe the strategy is right, if the agency people agree (because they all drew it up together), and if it can be shown that each ad is "on strategy," then there is no reason not to accept the campaign. So you see, far from being an enemy to creativity, a strategy can be the creative man's best friend.

first important question

So, there you are with your layout pad, your pens, and the product; you pick up the strategy and ask yourself: *Who are we talking to?* In my view, this is one of the most important questions you will ever have to ask as a creative person. The strategy answers it by defining the target audience. And you may find it written something like: "AB mothers between ages 25 and 45." I want to emphasize that although this is the target audience (to use professional jargon), it is not who you are talking to; rather, it is a *category* of person. What's the difference? Well, young to middle-aged women, with one or more children and husbands who earn between $15,000 and $65,000 a year, are a large spectrum of the population, and you cannot write ads to a spectrum.

Very often you will have a product that will appeal to millions; it's almost certain that the media you buy will reach millions; but when you get down to making your ad, you have got to be much more specific. You have to decide which of the families in that range of incomes ($15,000 to $65,000, remember) you think you are most likely to influence. Since you are talking to mothers, what effect will children have on whether they buy or not? Can you see, in your mind's eye, the type of woman who is most likely to be influenced by your ad? Can you hear how she talks? Can you devise an approach to your product that will make her listen? Is it possible that you have met one or two women who might buy the product? Could you name one of them? It is Mrs. Jones who lives just a couple of doors away? You're sure? Then *that's who you're talking to.*

talk sense

Now you wouldn't talk to Mrs. Jones as though she were a fool, would you? You wouldn't say anything to her in print, the sense of which you would blush to say to her face. In fact you would try to reason with her and show

Does the mortgage closing scare you?

Of course the "closing" scares you.

It scared your father before you. It scares everybody.

The mortgage closing is the last big step in buying a home. And you've heard tales about it. How you have to sign a lot of papers you don't understand. And write many checks for something called "closing costs".

You've heard that these costs are very high and completely unpredictable. And that before your closing is over you'll probably require medical attention.

True enough, you spend a lot of money at the closing. In fact, you're probably making the biggest investment of your life. But it doesn't have to be a harrowing experience.

Bankers Trust has found that when people know in advance what to expect, they survive their closings in pretty fair condition. So if you're thinking about buying a home, read on. Maybe you won't even need aspirin.

What is a Closing?

The closing is when you actually legally buy the house.

When money changes hands.

The bank lends you a large sum of money. You pass it over to the seller of the house (or his bank). He passes you his house.

You also give the seller a rather large check—the rest of your down payment. This may hurt a little but, after all, you're getting a house for it.

That, essentially, is the closing.

Those Horrible Closing Costs.

"Closing costs", strictly speaking, is a misnomer. There is only a "closing fee". The closing fee covers two expenses: the cost to the bank of processing your mortgage application, plus the fee for the bank's attorney.

At Bankers Trust, it costs you $110. This is the lowest closing fee of any major bank in New York.

The Shocking Part.

But don't get too happy yet, there are other expenses. The ones that take people by surprise. You pay these other expenses at the closing. But almost all of them are things you'd have to take care of anyway (even if you paid cash for your house).

For example, there's the land your house is built on. Do you know where your land is?

No you don't, it has to be surveyed (for a price). Just to be sure that the property you're buying is the same property you're getting. Then you have to record your deed to this property with the county (there's a fee involved, of course).

But remember, the land you're buying has been around a long time. And there is a possibility that in spite of everything, somebody may turn up who can prove that your house is on his property. This disaster could wipe out the bank's investment in you. So you must buy title insurance.

Property survey, recording fee and title insurance on a $20,000 home come to about $200. If it's any consolation, you pay this only once.

Your attorney may also recommend that you buy your own title insurance (the above only protects the bank). Should you decide to cover yourself, it'll be another $80.

Again, this is an approximate figure based on a $20,000 home.

One other potential disaster you and the bank have to be protected against is fire. Fire insurance for a $20,000 home costs in the neighborhood of $50. This is an annual expense.

And then, of course, there's the inevitable.

Taxes.

That Place Called Escrow.

Property taxes are a little complicated, and undoubtedly add to the reputation of the closing.

To figure out how much you'll pay for taxes at the closing, let's suppose you're buying your $20,000 home in New York City. At the N.Y.C. rate, your annual property tax will be about $660.

Once you're in the house, you'll be paying this tax in 12 equal monthly installments of $55 each.

At Bankers Trust, this sum is lumped in with your mortgage payments to the bank.

The bank sets this monthly tax payment aside in "escrow", which is a place you can't get at. The money is put in escrow because communities usually collect their property taxes only twice a year.

So the bank saves up six of your monthly payments and then makes a semi-annual payment of $330 to the community.

The closing gets complicated because it rarely takes place on the day a semi-annual tax payment is due. So a lot of figuring has to be done.

The purpose of the figuring is to decide how much you have to pay into your escrow account. So that by the time the next semi-annual payment is due, you'll have $330 in escrow.

Depending on the month you're closing in, you may even find yourself writing a check to the seller of the house, for taxes he's paid in advance. Or he may write one to you, for taxes you're paying that he should have paid. (Your lawyer really comes in handy at this stage of the proceedings.)

But enough of theory. How much does it come to in dollars and cents?

After all the paperwork settles

back on the table, you'll have paid between four and five months' worth of property taxes. In the present example, this would cost you between $220 and $275. You're not losing anything if you have to pay the higher figure; you'd have to pay it sooner or later anyway.

There's only one other large expense. New York State has a mortgage tax. It will cost you ½% of whatever your mortgage is. You pay it only once, fortunately, and now you're practically mowing that lawn.

Odds And Ends. And The End.

If the former owner has left some fuel oil in the tank, you have to buy it. (You'd have to buy oil anyway.) Figure $30.

And, of course, there's your lawyer's fee.

Living Happily Ever After.

If you get your mortgage from Bankers Trust, you'll be in a pretty good position.

Should you ever decide to prepay your mortgage (in whole or part) you can do so without the well-known "prepayment penalty".

And Bankers Trust will have offered you up to 25 years to pay off your mortgage. So the size of your payments should be comfortable.

And the paying is convenient. The bank handles the payment of all your property taxes and fire insurance. And, if you wish, you can arrange automatic monthly mortgage payments from your Bankers Trust checking account. At no charge.

Oh yes. Maybe someday you'll want to sell your house. Then you'll be on the other side of the table.

If that happens, be nice to the man who's buying it.

If he hasn't read this, he'll probably be scared.

You'll find a banker at Bankers Trust.

her a good argument as to why she should buy the product you have to sell. And because you know Mrs. Jones and how she thinks, you are in a much better position to know how to talk to her. You will speak sensibly, intelligently, with a smile here, a sound selling point there, all the time keeping her attention and making her feel pleased that you think she is worth all this time and trouble. Because you "see" Mrs. Jones when you write the ad, and not just a category of person, you are much more direct, much more personal, much closer to the right tone of voice to use.

> *If every copywriter knew who he was talking to when he made an ad, and could "see" that person as someone he had met, at once the quality of all advertisements would improve.*

Let's summarize what we have agreed on in this chapter so far. First, copywriting is not just a matter of having games with words; you have to put down a sensible case for a product. You have to direct that case to a target audience, which is defined in the strategy. But you never write to a category of person; you narrow your audience down to someone you actually know. And then you talk to that person, making sure you use the right tone of voice and speak with the right amount of intelligence. And when you have produced the ad, you have got a strategy to help you defend it when you present it to clients. You see, suddenly the craft is coming clear; it's not just a matter of ideas from the wide blue yonder (as I've said before); it's a matter of logic, common sense, and sound thinking.

second important question

Good, you now know who you are talking to, which, I repeat, is one of the two most important questions you must ask. The second question, equally important, is, *What do you want to say?* And again we turn to the strategy, where point two says: "What is the offer you want to make?"

You remember the example we used of the tire with a great number of sales points? And how we narrowed them down to one main thought, SAFETY? Well, a strategy should do just that for you: Narrow down the main thought. Which brings me to the title of this chapter: *Work on what to say.* And only after you are utterly certain of that should you concern yourself with how to say it. The style, the actual choice of words, the rhythm of your sentence, the pun if there is one, or the twist you are trying to work on a well-known phrase or saying—all that is a matter of style, or form, or *how* to say a thing. It is important, but only after you are totally clear on *what* you want to say. Because there is one thing utterly certain about making good ads:

You will never write an effective headline unless you find something effective to say.

The effect can be enhanced by the form of the words; the impression you create can be more forceful; you can get a promise remembered for longer. But no one will remember anything at all unless *what* you say is memorable.

if it sounds stupid when you say it, don't write it

Never be satisfied with a strategy unless it gives you something to say, and never write a headline, however literary, alliterative, or poetic, that says nothing. Don't worry in the first place whether your words are slick, polished, or trip off the tongue easily; ask yourself: What am I trying to say? Speak the promise out loud to the person you work with; that way you can tell if it makes sense, is part of the language of life, and stands up as an offer. And you will be able to tell, if you say it to your colleague's face and have in mind the person you are talking to, whether it is likely to be believed. It might be helpful at this point to go step-by-step through a case history, where I can name a real product and where we end up with a real campaign. Let us look at the advertising for Ryvita Crispbread. First, a little background to the product. Ryvita had been sold for many years as a good-tasting crispbread. It cost very little to buy, and was highly popular; everyone knew what it tasted like and most people were happy with the taste. But sales had reached a plateau.

The agency discovered that at the time there was a tremendous boom in the dieting market; sales of products to help people lose weight were rising dramatically. A few questions to the makers of Ryvita about the calorie content of the crispbread confirmed that not a single crispbread on the market—even those claiming to be starch-reduced—had fewer calories than Ryvita. Here was a chance to enter a booming market and extend the uses of Ryvita: by offering it as a way not only to enjoy a good-tasting food, but as an aid to dieters. The agency creative and account men got together to write a strategy:

Who is the target audience?
Women who want to lose weight.

What offer do we put to them?
Ryvita can help you lose weight.

What evidence is there that this is true?
No crispbread has fewer calories.

What final impression do we want to leave?
Ryvita really works.

Since this was a new business pitch, we didn't send the strategy to the client to get his agreement (which, you will recall, is usual practice if the agency already holds the account). We decided we would sell the potential client our strategy when he came into the agency to meet us and see our presentation, and we would then demonstrate that the advertisements interpreted it accurately.

So the creative people got to work, and the first question, if you remember, is *who are we talking to?* The strategy defined it as women who want to lose weight; so, did I know anyone who wanted to lose weight? Yes—Miss X. I know she has a healthy scepticism of advertisements, but she really does want to lose weight, and I think I can work on ways to get her to listen to an argument.

what interests miss x?

The most difficult problem is that she knows Ryvita of old and has never looked on it as a dieting aid. So I have to *change her attitude* and get her thinking this good-tasting bread is also a great help in trimming her figure. What are good ways to talk to 20-year-old Miss X? I know she is interested in fashions; that's one of the reasons she wants to lose weight. So I get some pictures of the very latest dresses from a leading London designer, and the models look really terrific, and I put a headline over each dress:

Like it? Ryvita will help you get into it.

This is a bit of a surprise, because I know Miss X has never considered Ryvita as a dieting bread; in fact, she's probably never though of Ryvita at all, apart from those times when she's munched a bit at the lunch table. So I have used the fashions to grab her attention, but at the same time I am making a good promise, and the ad is on strategy. Also, if I want, I can go on for years showing different dresses on different models but keeping the same headline. I have, in fact, got a campaign. I decided to give the idea the "overnight test."

THE INCH WAR

Making words collide is a good technique of saying something ordinary in an extraordinary way. The inch belt improves the headline. The pack is small because you don't need to tell people what a pack of Ryvita looks like. The copy starts with a fact. The baseline was subsequently changed from "Ryvita wants you to win" to "Ryvita helps you win." (Art director: *Paul Arden*)

There are over two million Britons fighting the inch war.

If you seem to be losing, Ryvita can help.

You need to eat fewer calories. No crispbread has fewer than Ryvita.

But you don't want to starve.

Ryvita helps you stave off that hungry feeling.

You do want to enjoy your diet.

The crisp, natural, nutty whole rye taste

of Ryvita sees to that.

Now perhaps you see why Ryvita is the most eaten crispbread.

It makes the inch war less of a fight.

Effective only as part of a calorie controlled diet.

Ryvita helps you win

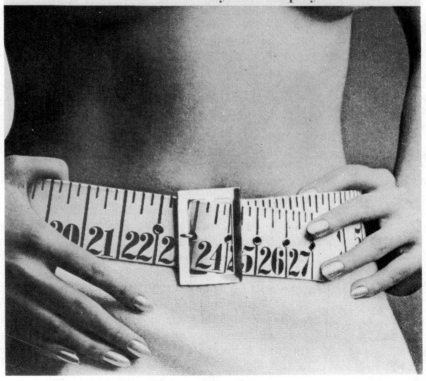

fatness or fitness?

What else is Miss X interested in? Well, I know she believes that one way she can lose weight is to do exercises; I've seen her wonder whether Yoga might help her figure; I know she's considered going to fitness classes (and so have millions of women like her). So I get some shots of a slender and pretty girl in a leotard, doing her exercises. And I put a headline over the upstretched arms:

Which slims best? Exercise or Ryvita?

Again this contains the element of surprise, and it's on strategy, makes a promise, and has enough life in it, showing different girls doing different exercises, to become a campaign. The problem is, how do I answer the question posed in the headline? I can't say Ryvita aids weight loss more than exercises, because Miss X simply won't believe me. But perhaps I can say that both Ryvita and exercises are equally good at weight loss. And provided I stress that Ryvita has to be eaten as part of a calorie-controlled diet and that I produce examples of women who have actually lost weight with Ryvita, there is nothing to stop this idea becoming a good campaign. I decided to give this idea the "overnight test."

Now do you see how these ideas were arrived at because I knew *who I was talking to*, and I knew *what I wanted to say.* Is it clear that, once you have an audience fixed in your mind, creative solutions suggest themselves? You know what pictures are interesting, you know what claims are believable, and you can judge the right tone of voice to use. And there is no worry about polishing the words in the headlines. Since I have decided *what* I want to say, it's easy to find the best, least tricky way of saying it.

Those two campaigns stayed on our walls for several days, but the question that kept coming back to me was: Were they surprising enough? Would they be strong enough to change the current attitude to Ryvita, which was that it was a homespun, good-tasting product? That was when I turned to technique. (Techniques are fully dealt with in the next three chapters.) Being absolutely certain *what to say,* I began to work on *how to say it.* I know that one thing I can do to build a good headline is make words collide. Which means putting a few words together that have never been put together before. Spend a few days considering the problem, and the brain can suddenly produce exactly the right phrase:

The Inch War. Ryvita wants you to win.

Now what I want you to take out of this case history is not the fact that there are a number of ways to go about creating a campaign (which, of course, there are) but the order of priorities. You must have a set way of working, or you will end up in that terrible haze of anxiety that is so unhelpful—wondering whether you should be in the business at all. You must have a system, and the one that I have found gives the best results is:

1. Agree on the strategy.

2. Decide who you are talking to (and remember that means pinpointing an actual person).

3. Decide what you want to say.

Only when all those things are absolutely clear in your mind should you work on the form the words take, which is why I have headed this chapter the way I have. When you know all about the product, can picture who you are making the ad for, and have honed down the product claim, then you turn to technique and make the final two or three ads to pin on your wall.

you can achieve greatness

I could go through several case histories, but the point about working within a system is always the same. And even if I describe *what* I did as closely as I can, what you really want to know is *how* I did it. When all is said and done, the would-be copy craftsman wants to know how to have an idea, and often simply describing ideas that have been arrived at is of no real help. It has been said that true creativity is something you are born with and that it cannot be taught; there may be a grain of truth in that. But it is quite incorrect to say that a young, inexperienced copywriter cannot be taught to become a first-rate craftsman; of course he can, and indeed, that is the aim of this book. What I would impress on you is that there is no profit in worry, and that you will never write the best work you can do if you worry over it; learning to work within a system helps prevent worry. Good copywriters can be made; they are not simply born. I don't mean that there aren't the odd one or two people in the business with a natural instinct for the work; of course there are. But most of us (and I include myself) have to be taught, and you learn by *getting priorities straight*. In fact, there are only two qualifications I would ask of the trainee writer: first, you must want to do the job; second, you must be willing to make sufficient effort to get results. If at first you don't succeed, you know what you have to do.

How you have an idea depends very much on what you do, which is why I have put so much stress on the practicalities of the job and have not dwelt, as yet, on the need for any inspiration. Every moment spent finding facts about the product, about the market, about the customer, and about what you want to tell him will pay dividends when you come to make your ad. Every fact can become a potential headline. Never try to speak to everyone; you will end up reaching no one. Dale Carnegie, who wrote *How to Make Friends and Influence People*, once said: "Why should anyone be interested in you, unless you are first interested in them?" If you want people to read, or listen to, and believe in your work, bear the question in mind.

Some Techniques

It will help you very much, when you are making your advertisement, if you know beforehand *how* it will be read. This matter has been the subject of much research, and the answers are quite specific. There is a definite route the eye takes over each ad. Let's say the reader is skimming through a newspaper or magazine. He turns the page, and there is your work, full of promise, waiting to catch his attention: What happens?

First, his eye goes to the picture. Then he reads the headline. Then he moves down to the bottom right-hand corner of the advertisement to see who is paying the bill. And, generally speaking, that is as far as most people get with most advertisements. As an aside here, it is worth mentioning that it has been estimated that in an average day, the average person has the opportunity to see between 1,000 and 1,500 different sales messages. It seems a lot until you remember how many posters you pass; how many buses with ads on them pass you; and how publicity is pouring out of radio stations, TV sets, and the pages of newspapers and magazines all the time.

cash down the drain

Of these 1,500 or so advertisements, the researchers estimate that the average man or woman remembers between seven and ten. The figures vary, depending on the company that conducts the research, when it's done, and where, but if you reckon that out of every 1,500 ads seen or heard, about ten make an impression, you won't be far wrong. These figures should give you pause for thought; it's obvious right away that a lot of advertisers are spending money and getting very little in return. It's also obvious how important it is to master the craft of ad-making, so that instead of doing work by so-called "instinct," you use the techniques available to make sure your ads get into the top ten.

Let us suppose you have caught the customer's eye; he's scanned your picture, headline, and logo and is still interested in what you have to say. Where does he look next? If you are using a squared-up photograph as your illustration, and if you have set a caption under it—possibly in a small italic face, as is used in a number of newspapers—the reader's eye will go to this caption next.

If you have still kept him interested, and if you have used cross-headings in your ad, or small drawings, charts, or graphs, the eye will scan over these next, picking out the salient points of your argument. Finally, if you have kept his attention throughout this eye-journey, and if he has been stimulated into wanting to know still more about what you have to sell, your reader will start on the body text proper.

That, according to the best research, is how people read advertisements. Now let us go back to the beginning and see what it can teach us about the craft of making ads.

use square pictures

People look at pictures before they read headlines. Surely then, the more of the story the picture tells, the more you will have communicated immediately. Later in this chapter I will list the 12 subjects that most make people read; knowing what they are will help you compose the kind of shots that get the most attention. Right now, it's worth remembering that newspapers and magazines most often use squared-up photographs. Since they are the kind of illustrations people are used to seeing most, and since they also offer you the best chance of good reproduction, you would be well advised to use them whenever you can. Cut-outs are quite unusual, so use them only when you have good reason.

the importance of headlines

The second stop on this eye-journey is the headline. As a copywriter, you should make no mistake: The headline is the most important part of your advertisement. If it doesn't communicate, your ad won't communicate irrespective of how powerful a picture you have used or how tastefully the layout has been done. I advise you to spend more time working on your headline than any of the rest of your words and to take great care over what the headlines says. One creative director I know says that any fool can write body copy, but it takes a real craftsman to create compelling headlines. (Certainly, if your headline is rejected, your ad is almost invariably dead.)

One point I cannot emphasize too strongly. There can be times when a headline does not need an illustration; but there can *never* be a time when an illustration doesn't need a headline. Of course you will see ads that go straight into the body copy from the picture: I call these ads "headless wonders." They are the occasions when the copywriter has copped-out. Advice to art directors—never let your writer make you run an ad without a headline. If he suggests it, tell him not to be so damned lazy. A great picture deserves a great line to back it up; even the painting of the Mona Lisa in the Louvre needs a small brass plate underneath reading "La Gioconda by Leonardo da Vinci."

HELP THE TWO OF US
Showing half of anything is a technique of making an ordinary picture look extra-ordinary. The headline means little or nothing without the picture. The copy was written only after visits to hospitals and talks with psychiatric nurses. (Art director: *Ron Brown*)

Help the two of us.

Becoming ill in the mind is not rare, nor frightening nor incurable.

One woman in six and one man in nine will go into hospital for mental treatment at some time in their lives.

Most recover and return to normal life. But while they are unwell they need nurses to care for them.

Life as a psychiatric nurse means you work at helping people come to terms with themselves.

The job is immensely varied as you have to be friend, counsellor, listener, observer and know a little about occupational therapy and social work.

You have professional status, responsibility and can work both in the hospital, and in the community.

Both men and women are needed.

If nursing hurt minds sounds like a job you might do well, please post the coupon.

ABOUT THE PICTURE. The problem of being 'in two minds', and thus finding a decision impossible, is a common trait in some mental disorders. The picture is symbolic of this.

Nurse the mentally ill.
A job for understanding people.

Please send me more facts about psychiatric nursing.

Name (Mr/Miss/Mrs) _____

Address_____

_____

_____

Age_____

To: The Chief Nursing Officer, Dept. of Health and Social Security, P.O. Box 702, London SW20 8SZ. (In Scotland, write to: –
The Chief Nursing Officer, St. Andrew's House, Edinburgh EH1 3DE.)

HELP KEEP NEW YORK CLEAN
You can judge a headline by how much it says, and this says a lot in five words. And
the words say something quite different from the picture. Sharing the work doubles
the impact. This ad is also written only for New Yorkers, who knew the product story.
(Art director: *Roy Grace*)

what makes headlines good?

First, they should always work *with* the picture. They should tell you one part of the story, while the picture tells the rest. Sometimes a headline can make no sense at all on its own. And a picture on its own can be a mystery. When the two come together, however, the whole story is revealed—with punch and originality.

Never use a headline to repeat what the picture is saying. And never simply illustrate a headline. *Let the two parts do their own half of the work*, so when you see them as an entity the story comes across quick and clear, the way it should on a poster. Every good ad should be able to stand as a poster; the reader should never have to dip into the small print in order to understand the *point* of the story.

Here is another fact research has discovered. The average reader spends about 1½ seconds on most advertisements. That's all the time you've got to shout: "We've got something for you!" And you must get the readers' attention in a manner that is *relevant* to your sales message. For example: You may want to write a headline: "Bags of Gold Free!" Now if the bags of gold *are* free, that's a good headline, but if you have to enter the competition to win them, or if they're only free if you go prospecting in the Rockies and dig the gold up yourself, then it's not a good headline. Any reader you have conned into the advertisement will feel very exasperated with you, and that irritation will be reflected onto the product you are trying to sell. As Leo Burnett once said: "I can get attention by having a man come downstairs with a sock in his mouth. But it's a rotten ad unless that sock is totally relevant."

apply polish and buff hard

Style is important when you write headlines. Not as important as content—*what* you say—but not to be dismissed as not mattering at all. One good tip to remember when you are polishing a headline is to throw out the present participle. "Watch sales *going* through the roof" can be trimmed to "Watch sales *go* through the roof" with no loss of meaning or impact. Ninety-nine times out of a hundred, the *-ing* is unnecessary in headlines (or body copy for that matter). It's a good idea to write in the present tense. However, never forget that when all the fancy pencil work is over, the effectiveness doesn't depend so much on the way you make your promise as on the promise you make.

We have covered some basic principles governing the picture and headline. (I say "picture" deliberately, because one picture is better than a lot of pictures. If you can simplify the shot to a single scene, your ad is working harder than if there are a number of different scenes.) The next stop for the eye is the bottom right-hand corner of the ad. This is where the client's name generally goes, as a signing-off note. Logo-types can speed communication here, but you can also use the space to wrap up the whole of your sales argument in a slogan. I'm not saying that every good ad should have a slogan; often a good case can be made for omitting a baseline altogether, but there are times when it can help. If you do decide to write one, try to see that it isn't just a mildly witty pun but that it urges the reader to go deeper into the ad.

tell what you can't see

The next stop in the eye-journey is at the caption under the picture. There are several hints worth remembering here. First, be sure to say something the reader can't see; never describe what the eye can "read" for itself anyway. Explain any action that is taking place. Name the characters you are showing, especially if one of them is a well-known personality. If at all possible, get the name of the product or service into the caption. If you have a black and white shot, indicating any important color can be useful. And finally, try to use the caption to direct the reader into the text. For example, a caption could be:

> *Harry Blank winning the world motor-racing crown. Read below how X oil helped.*

If you have used your techniques wisely and have kept the reader's interest so far, you'll have gotten over a great deal of information in a very short time. And every part of your ad has been earning its keep. Let us assume that the reader is still with you; he will then move onto your crossheadings and smaller illustrations. Make sub-heads punchy and factual. Facts sell—generalizations and puffs don't. If you use charts, make them simple and direct. If you have a small photograph tucked into the body copy, caption that as well, using the same techniques. In graphs and diagrams, use comparisons, name competitors, quote what experts or independent testers say, or use testimonials from satisfied users.

the smaller print

Finally, the eye reaches the beginning of the body copy. What are the best techniques to use here? Good body copy *starts in the middle*. Never begin by repeating any of the story the reader has already surmised. Go right to the heart of the proposition, and go with a punch. Never open with the name of the product—that's dull. Don't start talking about yourself; talk about the reader and his hopes and desires. And start with a flip: an up-beat phrase. I once read an autobiography that opened with the sentence: "Mom and Dad were married when I was three." How's that for inviting the reader to read on?

Remember that the whole purpose of the advertisement is to make people act, even if that action is simply to stop them thinking one way about the product and get them thinking about it in another way. To convince anyone about anything, you need more than specious or weak-kneed arguments and more than unsubstantiated claims and hyperbole. You need facts. Facts presented clearly, sympathetically, and with inexorable logic—and leavened with a little emotion—are best of all. Some people say that a copywriter is an *advocate* for his client's product. If that analogy is apt, the jury you have to sway are a hard-nosed bunch, not anxious to be parted either from their money or their opinions. If you talk to them in clichés, or waffle, or use superlatives that cannot be substantiated, they will dismiss the case without a second thought. You will be guilty of insulting their intelligence, boring them to death, and expecting them to hand over money for trash.

the wit to woo

The secret of a good advocate is that he gets attention and then tells his audience facts they don't know. He tells them in an interesting and unexpected way. He gets the listeners nodding in agreement; they say to themselves: "This man understands me, knows what I am looking for, doesn't treat me as a fool: I will give him a fair hearing." If people enjoy reading your work, they go on reading to the end of the ad. Moreover, some of that enjoyment will end up rubbing off on your client's products. Remember, too, you should never set out to write an ad without mustering all the facts. You can't be interesting unless you have interesting things to say, so unless your general knowledge is of a "Mastermind" standard, never rely on it alone to provide the information.

what makes people read?

You may have heard the old saying that there are only seven plots in the literary world. Countless stories, but seven basic plots. Likewise, there are only about a dozen subjects that make people read. And you will probably find ten of them every day in every popular newspaper. I hold the view that if you take any popular paper for one year, you will have read everything it's ever going to print. From year two, only the people, the places, and the numbers of the dead and wounded change. Certainly, I believe if all the world's news dried up tonight, most of our press wouldn't notice the difference. These dozen subjects get attention:

Animals	Fashion
Babies	Money
Cars	Sex
Disasters	Sports
Entertainment	War
Famous personalities	Weddings

The copywriter can use any of these subjects to help him get over his message. So if you have to talk to young women, you can reach them very simply by using a pretty baby. If you have to talk to young men, often a way to their hearts is through a racy car. I'm not saying that you can pin a subject to a product mechanically, or that originality has no place in your work—far from it—but simply that you will be a better craftsman if you know the techniques.

Here are some techniques you can use to write your ads. These techniques are also used by journalists and editors, who live or die by the number of readers they get. When an editor loses readers, he soon also loses his editor's chair. Advertising people may not be so harshly judged, but failure to make attention-getting ads results in a loss of job in the end. As I have said before, no good advertising is produced in a wild, haphazard, or undisciplined manner. The craft of copywriting has to be learned, and the learning involves knowing and practicing various techniques.

the *why* technique

WHY is an excellent word to use in a headline:

Why American commercials are better than British commercials.

Why I drive a Cadillac.

Brand X motor oil is best for your car. Here's why.

An explanation to my fellow managing directors why I must ask $205 for a pair of Brooks Brothers shoes.

The Inch War. Why Ryvita helps you win.

Why Sarah Jane gets the boys and Sally Anne can't.

And so there is a reward for reading. "Why" allows the copywriter to present a reasoned argument and list all the benefits the product has to offer. "Why" makes your ad *interesting.* Let me demonstrate.

Say a manufacturer comes to you with a new toothpaste that doesn't just shine your teeth, but also contains a really good mouthwash; so you may not need to use Listerine any more, or at least, not so often. Since that's a hard-to-beat sales pitch by itself, you could be excused for simply taking a picture of a pretty girl, with sparkling teeth, and punching out your promise in giant type: "We put a *mouthwash* in new Fresho." Your ad is clearly on strategy (it's probably quoting the strategy). You've made it plain who you're talking to and the promise comes out loud and clear. But clever and imaginative it isn't. And that is where "why" comes in.

Instead of the plain picture of the pretty girl, you photograph her this time with a man. Their arms are entwined; their eyes are locked together; their lips are open (to demonstrate some of that sparkle, of course). You could be excused for thinking they're on the point of a kiss (sex makes people read). All you do now is change the headline by one word: "*Why* we put a mouthwash in new Fresho." This time your ad is talking.

why adds fizz

Another example: Let's assume a car manufacturer has sold 10 million cars and wants to announce the fact. You're on solid ground to start with because you actually have something to say. No one could quarrel if you took a nice shot of the car, maybe being christened by a champagne bottle or something, and capped it with a bold headline: "Ten million Americans drive a Blank." On strategy, it makes its point, it is talking to drivers; but it's boring. But let's say the same ad was broken into various pictures that *demonstrate benefits* of the car; the way it corners, the way it economizes on fuel, the way it can carry a lot of people and luggage. You change the headline by one word: "*Why* ten million Americans drive a Blank," and your ad is immediately more interesting and more effective at doing a selling job.

Let me show you again. A manufacturer comes to you with a washing machine that has some good features, but a pretty stiff price. You decide to add some snob appeal and ask a well-known society lady to give the machine a testimonial. Then you shoot the product in a classy home, with the famous lady beside it and you say: "Annette Nuttie prefers a Brand X washing machine." OK, you've carried out the strategy. But judge for yourself how much more incentive there is to *read* the ad—even if you keep the picture exactly as before—if you rephrase your headline thus: "*Why* Annette Nuttie, who can afford any washing machine in the world, prefers Brand X."

If you simply want to make an announcement you say: "The men who invented the atom bomb now want to ban it." But if you've got to *make people read*, you preface all that with "why."

the *how* technique

I'd been in the business five years before someone pointed out to me the power of HOW. If your client offers a very complicated product or service and you have a lot of different points to make, "how" lets you go through them all. But there is virtually no limit to the number of ways the word will work for you.

"How to write a best seller in five minutes." Who could resist a headline like that (certainly not me, who saw it when I was at Chapter 4 of this book). In fact, it turned out to be promoting classified advertising space, and it went through the rules of writing good classified ads. "How to choose an advertising agency." That's a pretty compelling headline for a house ad, and any client new to advertising, or a touch unhappy with his present agency, is almost sure to pause. "How to choose the perfect stereo for your living room." A generic headline—that is, it could be used by any stereo manufacturer—but it should attract first buyers who want a stereo and don't know what they should look for. "How to spot a *lemon* car in a showroom." I just made that one up, but I know for sure I'd read it and so would anyone else who was thinking of changing his car. Don't these next lines demand that you read on?

How to read a banana.

How to have $25 extra in your pocket today.

How to cut your own hair.

How to turn the room in your head into a room in your home.

How to reduce your Income Tax by half.

The cleverest way I've ever seen "how" used was in conjunction with a stroboscopic photograph (that is, a picture where the image is repeated, each time in a slightly different position, so the shot actually records movement). The first image was of a puppy; then the images showed the dog getting older and older until the last one was of a fully grown animal. The artwork must have been compiled over the course of about a year, and you can imagine the impact that had. The headline simply said: "How to raise a dog."

the *where* technique

This is not so much the technique of using a word to begin your headline as thinking of *places* the product can be shown to its best advantage. Ask yourself questions such as: "Where will this product be most useful to the customer?" "Where will this product be least likely to work?" "Where will it perform at its best?" "Where is it most interesting?"

For instance: A client comes to you with a new kind of parka. He says it's amazingly lightweight but also totally windproof. You can show it to best advantage, and it's least likely to work, at the peak of Mount Everest. But that's where it's most needed. So you shoot a climber on the roof of the world wearing your client's product and have him say: "This is how I know Brand X parkas are best."

Oils are under most duress on race tracks, so that's where the commercials are based. A lady's foundation garment is least likely to be comfortable worn by a dancer doing a zippy dance routine, so that's where to demonstrate it. A safety belt is only useful in an accident, so that's where to show it. Say a manufacturer comes to you with a new wristwatch for women. Not expensive, but not unattractive either, and the selling point he wants to make is that it's waterproof. What about dropping it into a washing machine (one of those with a window in the front): "If you get into hot water, will your watch give you the time of day?"

the *who* technique

This is when you ask who can help you sell your product. It can include testimonials, but I want to deal with them under a separate heading, so let us look at "who" campaigns that are not simply testimonial ads.

TWENTY MINUTES HARD LABOUR

Here's a *who* campaign, featuring robots from space who mock humans for the time they waste preparing and cooking potatoes when an instant alternative (Smash) exists. The campaign had been running for years when this poster appeared, showing how the message can be reduced to "shorthand" once your audience is familiar with it. (Art director: *Dave Christianson*).

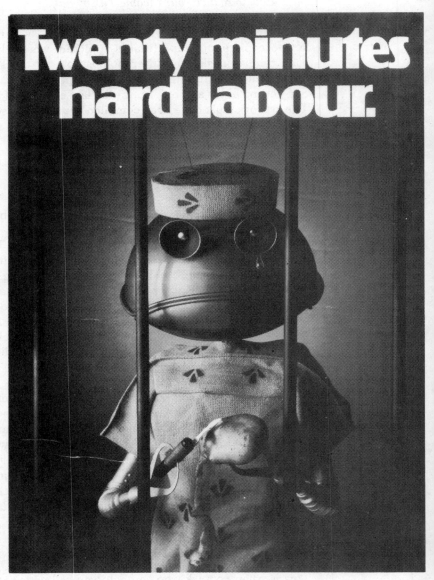

For mash get Smash in potato pieces.

You can use virtually anyone in a "who" campaign. Not just real living people, but characters from history (how many commercials feature Henry VIII?), characters from fiction (think of the commercials that have used Count Dracula, and numerous characters from mythology). One of the best ads I've seen in this category featured a happy little old lady, wrapped in a shawl and sitting in a rocking chair listening to a portable radio. The headline read: "What Mrs. Claus does on that one lonely night of the year!"

Nor need "who" be a human being. He can quite equally be a star-trekker (such as the robot in the illustration), a comic strip character (Superman is an example), an animal (the live bear in the Kelloggs Sugar Puffs films), or any of the characters that have been created and made popular by Disney and other cartoonists. I well recall a campaign for butter that featured Mickey Mouse, Donald Duck, and Goofy, to name but a few.

"Who" needn't be *one* character either. It can be a fictional family, it can be a group of workers in the client's factory (there is a marvelous ad that shows over 1,000 men in white coats standing around a VW Bettle, with the headline: "It takes this many men to inspect this many Volks-wagens"), or it can be any sports team, panel of scientists, or members of any group. As an illustration of the last category, I once used The London Philharmonic Orchestra to promote stereo. I went out and bought one of the orchestra's most famous recordings and invited the LPO to listen to it played on my client's equipment. I then asked how near to the live performance the recording had sounded and whether the intent of the conductor and players had been faithfully reproduced.

television actors

A popular technique these days is to invite a well-known TV personality to help you advertise. Although this can be very effective, it holds traps for the unwary. If you ever ask a comic to do a commercial, be certain he has a funny script. And don't expect always to be able to write that script yourself (you're a copywriter, not a scriptwriter). Arrange for his own scriptwriter to contribute the gags. If necessary, just hand over the sales point (or points) you want to make and ask him to write his own script around them.

If you hire a famous and beautiful actress to star in your film, don't think that she can carry it without a good idea. A top personality deserves a top creative idea to star in. Only then will you get full value for the vast sum you are probably paying.

If you do choose a TV personality, be sure he or she has a relationship of some kind to the product. It may only be that you want the star's personality to rub off on it: Check that it's the right kind of personality, because once you go through with it, it can last a long time. Finally, before we leave "who" campaigns, here is one ad that took the idea to its ultimate. It was for a catfood. The food was call "Miaow" (yes, cats asked for it by name), and the advertiser ran a campaign of grateful letters *from cats* commending the product.

the *when* technique

This entails asking questions such as: When will the product perform best? If you place your commercial *in the past*, will it be more effective? I've seen a beer launched on the slogan, "The lusty age is back," with characters in Medieval costume. Could you gain by having the film take place *in the future?* It was done very cleverly by an airline, who set their ads in the year 2001, when prices seemed astronomic. A vacation, they explained, was certainly more expensive than last year, but it was also cheaper than it would be next year.

The WHY campaign, the HOW campaign, the WHERE campaign, the WHO campaign, and the WHEN campaign are the five basic approaches to advertising. Literally interpreted, they will *not* make you a rich and famous copywriter. But knowing they exist as techniques will save you many unhappy hours sweating over a layout pad. Use the techniques intelligently; add your own 1 percent of inspiration and originality, going just that little bit further than the obvious without getting complicated, and you will make good ads.

More
Techniques

7

More
Techniques

We've looked at the five basic ways to approach a product; now let's look at some tried and proven techniques that will help you build good ads.

before and after

Remember the 98-pound weakling who always got sand kicked in his face? Then, one day, he starts on a Charles Atlas course (you too can have a body like mine), and next time he goes to the beach, all the girls are crazy for him? There you have probably the best-known before-and-after ad ever written.

Do you realize how often before-and-after is used? Bald men change into hairy heroes, fat ladies diet down to beanpoles, flat-chested blue-stockings develop Raquel Welch curves, dirty clothes come up bright and stain-free, matted woollens turn soft and lovely, even spotty glassware shines when you drop a little Finish into the dishwasher. These examples raise a smile—or at least an eyebrow—listed like that. They seem naive, even childish, and not in any way sophisticated enough to take in customers. Don't let the simplicity fool you: Before-and-after ads sell very hard.

The best campaign of this kind I've ever seen is one for Ayds Diet Candy. It was written by Ruth L. McCarthy, who even took a credit in the ads; and quite right too, because by giving herself a by-line, she explained why they read so beautifully when they were supposed to have been written by the dieters themselves. Take a headline like: "Watch me lose 80 lbs., a picture at a time," followed by a smaller sub-head: "By Mrs. Blank Blanko, as told to Ruth L. McCarthy." There follows half a dozen snapshots of a heavily overweight and poorly dressed housewife, who gradually loses inches and gains fashion sense until she's a trim lady with oodles of sex appeal. The captions under each picture give her weights in descending order. Then the payoff convinces you; if she can do it, you can do it. Before your very eyes you have visible proof of the efficacy of Ayds (and the skill of a top copywriter). There are countless other examples:

1. Two beefburgers side by side, one frozen, the other canned. Before cooking, they are the same size. After cooking, one has shrunk.

2. An unplayed phonograph record photographed through a microscope. The grooves are unmarked. The same grooves photographed after being played for 1,000 hours. The small amount of wear demonstrates the quality of the stylus.

3. Two car cylinders. One has been lubricated by oil without ingredient

WHICH IS THE CAT? WHICH IS THE COPYCAT?
Which twin has the Toni and which the expensive hair-do? Which hands belong to the Mother and which the Daughter (both are unmarked by housework)? Which shirt was washed by Daz and which with the pricey powder? If your pictures can *prove* your product is as good as the best anyone can offer, you've got an effective and convincing campaign. (Art director: *Roy Grace*)

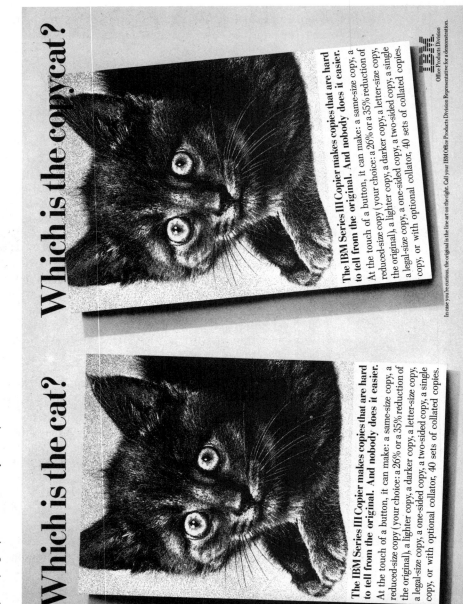

Which is the cat?

Which is the copycat?

The IBM Series III Copier makes copies that are hard to tell from the original. And nobody does it easier.

At the touch of a button, it can make: a same-size copy, a reduced-size copy (your choice: a 26% or a 35% reduction of the original), a lighter copy, a darker copy, a letter-size copy, a legal-size copy, a one-sided copy, a two-sided copy, a single copy, or with optional collator, 40 sets of collated copies.

The IBM Series III Copier makes copies that are hard to tell from the original. And nobody does it easier.

At the touch of a button, it can make: a same-size copy, a reduced-size copy (your choice: a 26% or a 35% reduction of the original), a lighter copy, a darker copy, a letter-size copy, a legal-size copy, a one-sided copy, a two-sided copy, a single copy, or with optional collator, 40 sets of collated copies.

IBM
Office Products Division

In case you're curious, the original is the line art on the right. Call your IBM Office Products Division Representative for a demonstration.

XK2. It is scored and dirty. The other looks almost new, since the same motor oil *with* ingredient XK2 cuts wear and gives more efficient driving.

4. Two plates of doughnuts before a kids' party. Mrs. X cooked one lot, Mrs. Y the other. Then the same plates after the party. Mrs. X's doughnuts have gone, Mrs. Y's haven't. Showing that Brand Z cooking fat, as used by Mrs. X, gives doughnuts more kid-appeal.

There's almost no limit to the changes you can ring on this old, but trusty, format; you can be serious and scientific or witty and light-hearted. Whichever approach you choose, done with any skill, you can be pretty sure you have a good ad.

invent a place

There's nothing new about this idea. The big retail stores do it every Christmas when they build fairy grottoes and install their private Santa Claus. Local authorities build model villages to attract tourists. Enthusiastic amateurs build model railways and a scaled-down countryside to go with them. And nowhere has it been done with more élan than in Disneyland, USA.

The copywriter can use the trick. To the best of my knowledge it was done first (and best) by Marlboro cigarettes, with their world-famous slogan: "Come to where the flavor is. Come to Marlboro Country." Today these cigarettes are the most popular brand on earth. But such a successful idea cannot escape the plagiarists. In the United Kingdom alone, at least four other advertisers stole the idea. Bird's Eye used it to sell their frozen vegetables, by showing them still in the fields, waiting to be picked. The pickers descend, and the crop is in the factory, and frozen solid within two hours. The campaign claim was that nowhere could you get fresher vegetables than from verdant, sun-drenched "Bird's Eye Country." A pretty blatant theft, don't you think?

This was followed by the UK Milk Marketing Board, who rechristened their pints of milk, "pintas." They began with the slogan "Drinka Pinta Milka Day" and went on later to feature cheerful children, playing in a cul-de-sac called "Pinta Street." Then a company called Butlins, who ran a chain of holiday camps, created a campaign promoting "Butlinland." The idea was that once you got to the camp you were in a new world, where everything was safe for the kids, comfortable for their parents, and a home-away-from-home for the Grandmas and Grandpas. All your troubles could be dropped at the camp entrance—at least for two weeks of the year. Then the makers of Haig Whiskey created Haigland, but the connection was so vague that I doubt if anyone ever understood the campaign. America too, followed Marlboro, and a seafood canner created his own ocean.

As an example of the life still in the idea, consider the campaign for the airline that wanted to promote vacations. To emphasize the choice they had to offer, the wide range of prices, the different lengths of stay, and the number of places, they called each of their offices *The Vacation Store*. Now isn't that a good place to buy a vacation?

invent a character

Think of the long-running campaigns that owe their lives to a fictional character. The eye-patched "Man in the Hathaway Shirt" has entered advertising lore. The Jolly Green Giant, and Speedy, the Alka Seltzer spokesman, also come immediately to mind. Speedy was around 20 years ago, disappeared when the advertising became more humorous and adventurous, and was revived quite recently in an attempt to boost Seltzer sales. In UK a stock-cube manufacturer sold his beef and chicken cubes for a generation through an imaginary family—the mother "Katie" gaining a husband and children as she and the campaign grew old together. And the Unigate company created an army of "Humphreys," striped straws that came out in the dead of night and stole milk from the ice box or anywhere else it was left around.

put the client in the ad

There is a neat little rhyme about what it takes to get approval for an ad, that goes something like this:

> *If the client moans and sighs,*
> *Insert the name block twice the size.*
> *If the man is still refractory*
> *Show a picture of his factory.*
> *Only in the direst case*
> *Should you have to show his face.*

That being said, there have been some excellent campaigns based on showing the client's face. One man who stole the show for a while was the late Commander Whitehead, a handsome bearded gentleman who looked like an ambassador, and who Schweppes used in exactly that capacity to introduce their products in the USA. Commander Whitehead was no photographer's model; he was a member of the Schweppes sales force, whose panache and sangfroid were used to persuade thirsty Americans of the qualities of Quinine Water and Bitter Lemon. I imagine that some of the buyers in the big chain stores even met him in the flesh, so to feature him in the ads as well was very shrewd. For a time, a Schweppes ad was empty without him.

Avis used the technique too—twice, in fact. Once they invited customers who wanted to complain to call the Avis president direct. You could reverse the charges and moan and groan at the very top man. There was a tiny caveat at the bottom of the page. It said, "If he doesn't answer after three rings, try later." I wonder how many times he got to the receiver that fast. The second time, Avis used their UK managing director. He made an appeal to the Avis staff to try even harder by publishing it in whole-page ads in *The Times* and other top papers. The gist of the story was: Avis is making big new promises to the public; please be certain we keep them. The ads impressed some people so much that they applied to Avis for jobs.

One last example should be enough to show you the changes you can ring on this idea. Company president, Mr. Frank Perdue, appears on American television explaining how much care he takes to raise good chickens and what rigorous standards he applies before he sells them. Mr. Perdue comes over as a pretty mean guy who works hard to make every Perdue Chicken as good as it can be. His slogan is: "It takes a tough man to make a tender chicken." Isn't it both flattering and reassuring to be asked to buy something by the president of a company?

give the product another name

The launch of the Volkswagen car into America has entered into advertising lore, and I have no intention of repeating any of the story here. But one of the techniques used to make the advertising succeed was to give the product another name, and because that name was based on the styling of the car, it seemed a natural thing to do. What *The Bug* also did was to add a whole new dimension of friendliness, humor and self-effacement to the ads.

You usually invent a new name to enhance produce benefits. For instance, Gillette once introduced a special safety razor blade. Its edge was sharper and made shaves more comfortable. The blade was called *The*

Spoiler: Imagine the impact of a headline like that with a hand holding a razor blade. The story explained how the blade spoiled your face *by babying it*. (And then you were spoiled for any other blade.)

Uniroyal built a new tire with road-gripping properties. People really started to want it, after it was christened *The Rain Tire*. Another tire company was the first in the United States to produce a radial tire. It was a me-too product (since the Europeans had been building radials for years) until they named it *The American Radial*.

You don't have to stop at renaming the product. You can rename the problem it's made to solve. For example, if you have a worse-than-average headache that needs quick relief, then you have *An Excedrin Headache*. Which is, of course, a headache that only Excedrin tablets can deal with. Or if you have an electric shaver for especially tough beards, a photograph of a chin in close-up, with the bristles looking really troublesome, can be headlined *The Human Jungle* to make the product's performance seem more exceptional. And when Iberia wanted to show off all the planes in their national airline, they headed their ad *The Spanish Armada*.

comparisons are excellent

There is no better advice I can give you as a copywriter than to say, if you have a better product, *prove it*. And there's no simpler way to do that than by comparison. You simply list the features your product has and prove, with a checklist, that your competitor doesn't have as many. Or you can compare performance figures and show your product works quicker, or more thoroughly, or lasts longer. Or you can compare the materials used to make your product and show, because you use better stuff to start with, that you can offer a better result. You can compare the number of times you inspect your product with the number of times other people inspect theirs. Or you can compare how a 20-year-old item remains perfect when treated with one product, as opposed to a similar item that has deteriorated.

You can compare the price anything costs to buy, the price it costs to run (over any length of time you choose), the price it will bring if you sell it again, and the price it will cost to replace if it goes wrong. You can compare maintenance costs, time needed to service, or the skill of the men you have to employ to put it right. So much for product, price, and performance.

You can also compare lifestyles. This is an especially useful technique in employment advertising, as these examples show. The London Police proved that cops led more exciting, varied, and responsible lives

Some beefburgers always seem to lose something in the cooking.

Frozen.

Before they were cooked, there wasn't much to choose between the beefburgers above.

Then, alas, the frozen one shrank. So we cooked a few more.

It happened again. And again.

It seems with some beefburgers you cook, you always end up with less than you expect.

Not so with our canned beefburgers.

There's a full rib in every can. They don't come in gravy as some people believe.

And they never promise a meal, then end up a snack.

That's Heinz.

Once a big burger, always a big burger.

Bigger Beefburgers from Heinz.

Heinz.

SOME BEEFBURGERS LOSE SOMETHING IN THE COOKING

If you want to give your competitor a good knock, compare his product with yours. Then prove the claim that yours is better. Tell in the copy what you don't immediately notice in the picture. This ad couldn't have been made without facts. (Art director: *Peter Harold*) than the average man in whole-page ads that asked: How does a week in your firm compare with a week in ours? The nursing profession proved they could offer more job satisfaction by showing a distinguished consultant discussing a case with a trainee nurse. The headline read: "Did anyone at work ask your opinion today?" The nurses also demonstrated how your social standing improved when you joined the profession by showing a nurse, back-view, with the headline: "What do people say about you behind your back?"

You can be sure comparison advertising is effective because it is so controversial. Some people will not have it at any price and denigrate it by calling it "knocking copy." There may be a case for not knocking competitors because they can knock you back harder. My own view is that if you compare like with like, avoid misleading your audience, and don't draw conclusions that can't be justified, it is good salesmanship and common sense to do comparative advertising. After all, comparing is what every sensible customer should do before buying anything.

the challenge

This is a technique that crops up every so often, especially to launch a new product. The idea is that the new product *challenges* others on the market and says things such as: If you can find a better version of this product, we will give you back the money you spent on ours. Some manufacturers go even further and offer to pay for the alternative that's been found as well. But of course only after they have examined that alternative, agreed it really is superior, and the customer has provided proof of what he paid for it. Challenging slogans include: If you can find a better bourbon, buy it. If you get a better deal downtown, we'll match it. Never knowingly undersold.

the guarantee

This one is tricky because most of the public is now aware that a manufacturer's guarantee can deprive them of some of their rights, and that they can be worse off signing it than ignoring it altogether. If you do decide to produce a guarantee, you would be wise to say at the beginning (if your client will agree to it) "This guarantee in no way deprives you of your rights under the various consumer protection bills." As for the rest, try to be specific in the items you guarantee, include as much detail as possible (without becoming unreadable), and be sure to stipulate where the manufacturer is accepting more responsibility for the life and performance of

What do they say about you behind your back?

You probably won't hear people say these things.

They'll likely whisper them from bed to bed with you just out of earshot.

But if you become a nurse, the comments that follow will be almost inevitable.

"She's so understanding."

And since you'd never have taken the job unless you liked people, it's understandable they'd say that.

But nursing develops that trait.

It trains you to watch and listen, and think about your observations.

It's not just a matter of being nice. It's doing your job better, so that the people in your care recover more quickly.

"Isn't she confident?"

Yes you will be.

And it will be a confidence based on hard work.

We'll teach you exactly what to do, and tell you why you're doing it, and how it helps.

This complete understanding of the job brings self assurance.

Which you, in turn, pass on to the patients.

Your training is based on many years of experience and millions of case histories.

No wonder it works.

"She's young for the responsibility."

That's probably true.

No other job would have you observing in an operating theatre at nineteen.

Or dispensing dangerous drugs or joining a cardiac arrest team before you reach twenty.

We don't believe teenagers are only fit to dial 118 and make tea.

We believe that given the right supervision you can rise to the occasion.

You'll work with head, heart and hands. And with a senior never too far away.

"I wish I could be as efficient."

The whole of your training teaches you to make the most of your time and effort.

In the case of a cardiac arrest four minutes can make the difference between full recovery and permanent brain damage.

Do you think we can afford to let you do anything in a haphazard or unplanned way?

And if you take this efficiency

into your private life after you leave work, so much the better.

"How does she keep so cheerful?"

This can be hard, especially if someone has just died on the ward.

(Yes, you have to face the fact you are in a profession that deals with life and death.)

There's plenty of reason to be happy when newborn twins appear on the scene.

The knack of acting relaxed, cheery, unruffled is probably learned from the people who've nursed for years.

But it's an invaluable side to any personality.

Are we making you think more seriously about a career in nursing?

If so, why not make enquiries at your local hospital.

Alternatively, drop a line to the Nursing Association.

The Chief Nursing Officer, Dept. of Health and Social Security, PO Box 702, London SW20 8SZ.

**Nursing.
It's not just your own life
you make the best of.**

WHAT DO THEY SAY ABOUT YOU BEHIND YOUR BACK?

How to talk to teenage girls. And in doing so, prove that you can offer them more responsibility and improved status in the community. Here the picture tells you what job is being advertised. Show this ad to anyone who tells you not to ask questions in headlines. (Art director: *Paul Hanson*) his product than he has to under the law. There is evidence that if any mail-order ad includes a guarantee, sales are almost certain to be higher.

the torture test

This is one of my own favorites, first, because it can add excitement and showmanship to your campaign; second, because torture tests, by their very nature, prove the efficacy of your product; and last, because they are not hard to think up. The case of the climber selling the parka from the top of Mount Everest was a kind of torture test, as was the watch in the washing machine. Here are some others I've used in campaigns.

To demonstrate the efficacy of a self-cleaning oven, we had it painted inside with a mixture of cooking fat, sugar, and raspberry jam, which was slowly baked hard onto the oven walls. The "after" picture showed the oven spotless again, untouched by human hands, and for a cost of about five cents.

We had a letter from a disc jockey who had stayed awake for seven days and nights, playing non-stop music to get into the *Guinness Book of Records*. The point of his writing was that he had used a stereo set that we were advertising. It led to a very nice shot of an exhausted DJ flopping over the stereo, with the headline: "After playing for 168 hours non-stop, a vital part failed."

One client I wrote for introduced an aerosol bath cleaner and an aerosol window cleaner. We produced a commercial using the first to clean the sides of a white ocean liner and the second to polish the biggest window in the world (which, if you're interested, is fitted on the front of a horse-racing stadium in Kentucky).

Don't wait for your client to suggest torture tests: Dream up your own ideas and suggest them to him. He'll soon shoot them down if they won't work; and if they do work, they make interesting as well as convincing copy.

when words collide

I said a little about putting words together in an unexpected way in Chapter 4, when we looked at The Inch War campaign. It's not out of place to emphasize again here that before you try this technique, you have to decide what you want to say. The effect of seeing words in collision (so to speak) doesn't happen unless they communicate something. For example,

I could write CABBAGE SKY and put two words together for the first (and, I hope, last) time, but since they don't *say* anything, you will simply reject them as nonsense. However, once you know what you want to say, colliding words is part of the *mechanics* of saying it. Everything will become clear as we look at some examples:

> *Soft whisky*
> That sounds a nice idea, doesn't it?
>
> *Slow ketchup*
> Hmm. I suppose they mean good and thick.
>
> *Central heating for kids*
> A nice hot breakfast cereal.
>
> *Try this thirsty hair test*
> Eh? Have *I* got thirsty hair?
>
> *Bananas: 45 cents a foot*
> They must be joking (the bananas were inflatable).
>
> *The Tuesday drink*
> Never heard of it, but it might be nice.
>
> *Table whisky*
> Ah, that's the one good enough to have out
> on the table when guests arrive.
>
> *The down-home taste*
> That's the taste you feel relaxed and at home with.
>
> *Pyjamier pyjamas*
> You mean they make me feel ready for bed.
>
> *Make a slap-up supper slapper upper*
> I'd like to; tell me about the product that does it.

The great thing about these phrases is they're *unexpected.* That quality makes them seem to be new when some of the products they talk about are old. They make people read.

You can try the same game with letters. *Drinka Pinta Milka Day.* This is a totally different matter than saying: "Drink a pint of milk each day." *Beanz Meanz Heinz.* What a terrific line for a market leader. *Wotalotigot.* Written in kiddy scrawl, it's a way of saying you get a lot of chocolate beans in one tube. I don't need to point out that large appropriation, long-running campaigns have been built on all these slogans.

finally, some key words

There is a school of thought among copywriters that says originality comes before all, and although it is no part of my aim to decry originality (indeed I applaud it), I will not accept the corollary that because some words and pictures are used a great deal, they won't bear further repetition. Here, I would like to make it clear that I lay down no rules. There is only one rule about making ads, and that is, there are no rules about making ads. But some words and phrases we know are *buzz* words. They provoke a reaction. They include: now, free, introducing, announcing, secret, magic, mother, unique, money off, save dollars, sent direct from the manufacturer, economy, bargain, breakthrough, guarantee, and offer closes today.

I could go on, but that bunch is enough to give you the idea. They are action words, and the only qualification to using them is you should make sure they are appropriate. The argument runs, you see, that through frequent use they have become clichés and are, therefore, devalued. Although it is true that they are clichés, they still keep their value, as the sales returns never cease to verify. Why they keep their power, I don't know, just as I don't know why people will go on reading newspapers that print the same cycle of stories year after year. But I am sure—and you better believe it too—they *work*.

Still More
Techniques

You may now have an impression, after the last two chapters, that making ads is mechanical. Not so. There is a parallel in painting. First you learn the craft: how to mix the colors, how to use the brush, how to capture a likeness, how thick or thin to lay on the paint to give a precise result. Then you practice the skills. It's when you are able to add your own inspiration that painting becomes art. And it's when you add originality to technique that ad-making becomes creative. So, more about the craft.

contests

The best headline I ever saw on a contest ad was: "For once in your life, enter a contest." That line recognizes that, generally, people feel they haven't a chance in a million of winning a contest, so most of them never bother to try. The others, who feel they can win, are often professional contest-doers, and they have perfected the knack of writing tiebreakers. You see, even if a contest is as simple as an easy math problem, everybody knows that you're going to catch them when it comes to: "Say, in not more than a dozen words, why you love Brand X."

Are contests worth considering, then? Yes, on two counts. First, they can be a very good way to change the pace of your advertising. Let's say you have a long-established product, with a reasonable sales graph, but somehow it seems to be becoming a part of the wallpaper. If you want to get it back into the public consciousness for a few weeks, plan a contest. The only proviso is, you should have an amazing prize.

Be the chairman of our board for a month.

Own shares in every company on the Stock Exchange.

Rob a jewelers. Keep all you steal.

Stay a week in the Arctic with Eskimos.

Have Alice Neel paint your portrait.

Own your own pub.

This last offer comes from a highly successful campaign in UK. Most British pubs are owned by the brewers, but are run by managers or tenants. The advertising was addressed to these two groups, most of whom would be delighted to own the freehold of the premises, and so enjoy all the profits, instead of only part of them. When a pub is owned by an individual, it can choose the brewers from whom it buys its stock, and so becomes known as a "free house."

The campaign run by a soft-drink manufacturer offered to buy a pub outright, and give it to the tenant or manager who sold the most of his product over a given eight-week period. The advertisements featured several "free houses" available, tenants who were ahead at a particular time, different ways of gaining points, and, a week before the contest closed, a bonus scheme to give laggards the chance to catch up. Clearly, it produced a deal of enthusiasm, and many publicans enrolled their customers in the effort to drink more.

When the contest closed, the organizers threw a party. The winner was given the keys to his own pub, and runners up received generous consolation prizes. Then the plans for *next* year's contest were announced. An appetizing outline was sketched, and publicans were reminded to keep in touch with the company salesmen, who would supply them month by month with the important details. The contest achieved three things—a great deal of interest and goodwill for the manufacturer, an audience ready and waiting to see the salesmen throughout the next trading year, and, of course, a real lift in the number of soft drinks sold.

The second way to use a contest is to get trial purchases for a product. Say you've got a new line (or an improvement to an old line) and you want a lot of people to try it as quickly as possible. Hold a contest which people can enter only if they send in *proof of purchase*. The way to succeed this time is *not* to offer one big imaginative prize, but thousands of smaller ones, to persuade as many people as possible that they have a reasonable chance to win. (A first prize in a contest like this can't be big anyway, since budgets will never allow it; that scarcely matters if you have, say, 10,000 runner-up prizes.)

The good thing about the second type of contest, from the public's viewpoint, is that it may be possible to forego the tiebreaker; or if you do have to have one, then it can be easier to complete. The bad thing, from the manufacturer's point of view, is that you have to spend a great deal of time and trouble organizing the judging. Nevertheless, one advertiser I know who ran the second type of contest got half-a-million people using the product in three weeks.

mr. ferrari drives a fiat

Or so I'm told, by the ad I'm looking at now, which is an excellent example of another technique: the testimonial from your competitor. Now it's unlikely that a direct competitor will plug your goods, no matter how much you pay him, but since the man who buys an expensive Ferrari and the man who buys a cheap Fiat are almost certain to be different animals, it's no skin off the sports car maker's nose to say nice things about the family car.

Even if you don't have a specific name to drop in your ad (and it's obviously better if you have), you can still use the basic idea.

The kind of loaf the baker's wife prefers.

Where travel agents take their vacations.

Why most car mechanics choose a Volkswagen.

What other tailors admire about our suit.

France's top wine taster tells how to choose coffe.

topicality

At one time you could only be topical in the press, since only the press could take copy at very short notice. Then videotape came along; and now you can have a commercial for motor oil on TV only hours after a driver who uses it has won the World Championship. The benefits of being topical?

1. It's a way to change your pace.

2. It's a way to borrow interest from news, fashion, sports, or current events.

3. It can help the advertiser seem more human.

4. It can let you be very funny.

Topical ads come in two categories. In the first, the advertiser ties in with an event directly connected with his business; for example, a parka maker with men who've just conquered a high mountain, or a camera maker with a current photographic contest. In the second, product and event have no apparent connection.

1. In Britain, when the Post Office raised their stamp prices (again), Volkswagen ran an ad showing new-value stamp flanked by a VW symbol with the headline: "They are still two of the cheapest ways of crossing the country."

2. When the Stock Exchange Index in New York reached 1,000 for the first time, Johnnie Walker ran an ad quoting the figure with the headline: "Congratulations to those who had the guts to stay in."

THEY ARE STILL TWO OF THE CHEAPEST WAYS
OF CROSSING THE COUNTRY
Here's how to make a picture really work hard. And be topical. And change the
pace of your advertising. Note how this ad builds on all the other VW ads that
have appeared before it. Lesson: You very rarely advertise in a vacuum. (Art
director: *Derrik Hass*, from an idea by *John Knight*)

They are still two of the cheapest ways of crossing the country.

This is a timely reminder from VW that a Beetle can do 38 miles to a gallon of 3 star.
40,000 miles to a set of tyres. Often 100,000 to an engine. That it never needs anti-freeze. Hardly ever needs oil. And holds its value like few others in Glass's Guide.

So that even at £989 for a basic model, a Beetle's a bargain.

So is a new 3½p stamp, if it's used properly.

If you stick one on an envelope and address it to Volkswagen (GB) Ltd, Volkswagen House, Purley, Surrey we'll send you a Beetle brochure. Absolutely free.

Few things in life work as well as a Volkswagen.

Recd retail price VW 1200 £989 inc VAT and Car Tax Delivery seat belts number plates and currency exchange surcharge extra
VOLKSWAGEN GB LTD. VOLKSWAGEN HOUSE BRIGHTON ROAD PURLEY SURREY TELEPHONE 01-668 4100 A MEMBER OF THE THOMAS TILLING GROUP

quizzes and tests

How well have you read this book? Test yourself.

1. Where should the product be when you write an ad?
2. What's so helpful about an advertising strategy?
3. What technique is used when an ad features a movie star?
4. What single word is most likely to increase readership?
5. Name three subjects that make people read.
6. Of the 1,500 ads seen daily, about how many register?

The quiz (or test) technique is a favorite with editors. Think back to how often you have checked to see how good a lover/husband/wife/driver/parent you are? Since the format is so hard to resist, use it in ads, too, but with a word of warning. This kind of ad is almost always generic; the headline can apply to almost any product in the category, so unless you really are stuck for something to say, you should try to be more specific.

range advertising

As a general rule, putting a range of products into one ad is a *bad* idea. Because:

1. People never buy a range.
2. The time to say there are variations in your product is *after* you've convinced me I should buy the general concept.
3. Equal emphasis on many products means scanty treatment for them all.

I advise you to either persuade your client to spearhead only one of his range or to feature the different variations in separate ads.

If the client does agree to spearhead one model, the question then arises, which? Generally, the answer is the one that sells best. Or failing that, the most expensive, because it presents the product-type at its best, and any glamor and style can rub off onto the cheaper models.

If you're dealing with the fashion trade apply a different rule: By all means spearhead your most popular line, but also take one ad to show your most outrageous garment. When a fashion editor looks at the

JUST A REMINDER THAT THE MOST IMPRESSIVE THING ABOUT CHIVAS REGAL
IS WHAT'S IN THE BOTTLE, NOT WHAT'S ON IT
Occasionally a creative team finds a new way to exploit the product label. Drinkers
"sang" it in Carling commercials. In UK they read it in a Cointreau film. VAT 69 ran a
poster with the number painted out (Headline: Think of a number). Here's the Chivas
version. (Art director: *Bill Harris*)

**Just a reminder that the most impressive thing about Chivas Regal
is what's <u>in</u> the bottle, not what's on it.**

12 YEARS OLD WORLDWIDE · BLENDED SCOTCH WHISKY · 86 PROOF · GENERAL WINE & SPIRITS CO., NEW YORK, N.Y.

season's creations, she goes for the zany, the wild extravaganza, to put in her column. It may be true that only a very few customers (maybe none) will ever buy that garment. But they'll say: "Did you see that marvelous dress by so-and-so?" And they'll feel great if they can tell you they are also wearing a so-and-so creation, albeit in a much more conventional style. When the House of Schiaparelli re-opened in Paris in 1977, designer Serge Lepage offered a white chiffon dress with 512 diamonds sewn into it. Price?—two million dollars. I don't know if he found any buyers, but he certainly won a lot of publicity.

What about the techniques for making range ads? There are at least two. One is the *guide technique*:

For a range of girdles and bras: "Every girl's guide to a lovelier Silhouette."

For a range of haircuts: "Your guide to the hairstyle that best suits your face."

For a range of frozen foods in winter: "Your guide to the week's best vegetable buys."

The other is the *what do you want most?* or the *which is right for you?* approach. Here, you group the products according to the qualities they offer and invite readers to decide which variation suits them most.

quotations

This is often the place where the trainee copywriter starts—and believe me, it's a mistake. Famous poets and dramatists rarely have much to say about selling. There may be times when an apposite quotation works better than anything else, but they are few and far between.

Here are two instances where quotations were right. When the US Government was urging Americans to come to the polls in 1969, one ad summed up the message with a quotation from Edmund Burke: "All that is necessary for the forces of evil to win in the world is for enough good men to do nothing." Who could refuse to vote after that warning? And when Britain's Christian Aid wanted to push home their belief that a helping hand is better than a hand-out, they said: "Give a man a fish and you feed him for a day. Teach a man to fish and you feed him for life." When you think of the number of advertisers asking for charity these days, you won't find many better reasons to give than that.

All that said, when I began as a copywriter, I wasted many hours looking through Roget's *Thesaurus* and the *Dictionary of Quotations*, hoping those books would lead me to good headlines. It never happened! Much better to follow the routine from Chapter 2: study the product, study your market, get all the facts you can, decide who you're talking to, then *think*.

demonstration

Showing the product at work is one of the most common (and most effective) ways to sell. It is best when you have sound and music to help you, which means making a film. But it is also possible to demonstrate in press, either with stroboscopic pictures (the ones that capture movement), sequences of photographs (before-during-after), or with diagrams. For example:

> *Four pictures each captioned with a time: 8 a.m., 8:01 a.m., 8:10 a.m. and 8:11 a.m. In the first picture, a man is standing beside the open hood of a car holding a hosepipe. In pictures two and three the hose is pouring gallons of icy water into the engine. In picture four, the car is driving away. Headline: "A little moisture in the atmosphere won't stop a Volvo." Not quite as effective as it would be if you saw a film of water splashing over points and plugs and gushing round the distributor, but effective enough.*

If you *are* working on a film, there are four basic ways to go:

1. *Show and Tell* The best British example of this technique in recent years is the TV commercial for the Black & Decker "Workmate." We see that versatile tool put through its many practical uses (saw-bench, step ladder, vise, and so on), and the film ends by showing how neatly "Workmate" hangs away on a garage wall. No tricks, no star actors, no silly jingles, just straight voice over, telling you what you see and how much you have to pay. Excellent selling.

2. *Slice of life* Action in this kind of film opens and ends on "real-life" situations, but in the center of the film, the advertiser drops in a demonstration; for example, open on housewife holding her head.

Husband: Headache, dear?

Wife: Something dreadful.

A LITTLE MOISTURE IN THE ATMOSPHERE WON'T STOP A VOLVO
Here is a demonstration and a torture test combined. Plus a picture that proves the claim being made. And how's the headline for understatement? (Art director: *Phil Mason*)

A little moisture in the atmosphere won't stop a Volvo.

What you see happening in the photographs actually happened.

The Volvo started first time, leaving behind a relieved photographer and a smiling spokesman from Volvo.

Not that anyone should have been surprised.

The vulnerable parts of the Volvo engine, like the plugs and distributor, are well-protected from the elements.

Come rain, hail, sleet or snow, a Volvo is expected to start.

In Sweden, temperatures can be sub-zero for 6 months in the year, and being stranded on a country road within the Arctic circle isn't quite the same thing as waiting for the AA outside Cheltenham.

The Volvo 244 is reliable because it has to be. And because it's built to be.

It takes a Volvo nine hours to crawl through the final assembly plant.

And in a factory where engineers outnumber stylists by 40 to 1, each car is minutely examined.

But if you're looking for statistics to back up our reliability claim, one seems more convincing than any other.

92% of Volvo owners intend to remain Volvo owners when they next change their car.

And as evidence goes, we'd say that was pretty reliable. **VOLVO**

For your free copy of "The Volvo Facts" write to: Volvo Concessionaires Limited, Lancaster Road, Cressex Estate, High Wycombe, Bucks. HP12 3QE. Tel: (0494) 33444.
Export enquiries to: Volvo Concessionaires Ltd., 26 Albermarle Street, London W1X 3FA. Tel: (01) 493 0321.

Husband: You need two Blank tablets. Dissolve to transparent plastic model of human head. Dotted arrow animates from mouth to back of head while voiceover explains that Nothing acts faster than Blank. (OK, I'll have Nothing.) Dissolve back to wife, now smiling.

Husband: You look better now, dear.

Wife: Oh yes, Nothing acts faster than Blank.

And we cut to a close-up of the pack, two tablets, and a title. I know it's a cliché and utterly boring, but you see films like it on TV almost every week in winter, so they must be doing something right (mustn't they?).

3. *Trick Films* This is exactly what it says, using cinema tricks such as slow motion so the audience can see what usually happens too fast for the eye to follow. Or repeating a few frames over and over again to emphasize a point. Or reversing the film. Or changing from color to black and white (or vice versa) for the demonstration sequence. Or by shooting through a microscope, or using X-ray shots, or any other device that can help you prove a point.

4. *Animation* This is where it's impossible in practical terms to film the product in action. Say you have a tire that stays inflated if you get a puncture at speed. You can't film it patching itself from the inside, but you can explain using animation. By the same token, you can't wait around filming how the action of plaque causes tooth decay. But you can simulate it well enough through animated drawing.

The keynote of demonstrations is simplification: Say it clearly, say it believably, and don't leave any loopholes.

a lot can happen in a day

Using the word "day" can help you produce a slogan. Here are six slogans from current and past campaigns in America and Britain.

Mennen adds go to the day.

Cadbury's Chocolate. One of today's great tastes.

A Mars Bar a day helps you work, rest, and play.

Make the day with Cadbury's Milk Tray. (another chocolate bar)

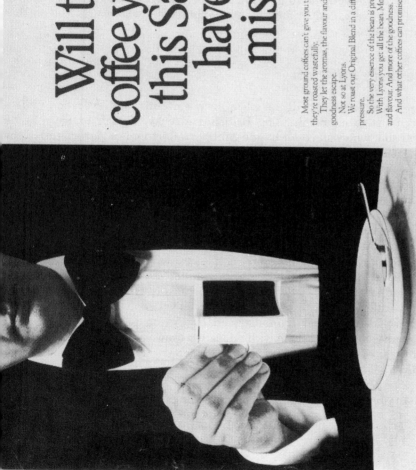

Will the real coffee you serve this Saturday have part missing?

Most ground coffees can't give you their all, because they're roasted wastefully.

They let the aromas, the flavour and other coffee goodness escape.

Not so at Lyons.

We roast our Original Blend in a different way. Under pressure.

So the very essence of the bean is preserved.

With Lyons you get all the bean. More of the aromas and flavour. And more of the goodness.

And what other coffee can promise you that?

Fresh Ground Coffee
Roasted Under Pressure

WILL THE REAL COFFEE YOU SERVE THIS SATURDAY HAVE PART MISSING? Remember "Help the two of us?" Here's another example of how cutting something in half adds impact. It turns the expected picture into the unexpected. The whole campaign was based on a fact that came to light only after talks with the Lyons chief coffee blender. (Art director: *Paul Hanson*)

Spend a day with the Princess. (The Princess was the name of a sportily-designed saloon car made by British Leyland.)

Bournvita puts back what the day takes out. (Bournvita is a hot malt drink, made with milk, to be drunk at bedtime.)

So we can learn two things: first that the word "day" can add weight to a slogan. And you can make a good ad if you base it on a day in the life of the product. There are other uses too. The Saturday Shirt was a very good brand name for a range of leisure shirts. The Tuesday Drink formed the basis of a campaign for whisky. (The story was you could drink it whenever you liked, but you *had* to have some on Tuesdays.) And I offer the idea of an aftershave called Friday to any manufacturer who wants it. (Get that Friday feeling, every day of the week!)

the strip cartoon

There is no one who doesn't like strip cartoons, and everybody has a favorite strip character. The British are lucky enough to have Frank Hampson, who was voted by the American Cartoonists Association to be the best writer and artist of strip cartoons since the end of World War II. (This was at the University of Rome, in 1975.) Strip advertising is a natural for kids' comics—DC's Superman almost always has a page on bubble gum or similar products, but it needn't be used only for children's products.

Government estimates say the UK has nearly two million barely literate adults, and since the US population is three times that of the UK, America must have even more. Strips are a great way to reach them. They're also good to show how a product should be assembled, dismantled, or used, or to *demonstrate* in press advertising where movement is not available. But strips can also be used with considerable subtlety, as a drink manufacturer demonstrated by buying pages in UK women's magazines and filling them with delicately drawn pictures that lifted them well clear of the banal. There are two guidelines: The first is to decide who you're talking to. The second is to make certain you use a first-rate artist. Drawing strips is not as easy as it looks. Nor is writing them, because you mustn't repeat in your words what the picture is clearly telling.

Television

Most, if not all, of the techniques covered in the last three chapters can be used whether you are making an ad to appear in the press or on the large or small screen. But since paper and film are two very different media (David Bernstein, in his book, *Creative Advertising*, actually lists 29 points of difference between them), I have given film a chapter to itself. There is only one difference I want to stress—and I freely acknowledge it is included in Bernstein's list:

1. A newspaper ad cannot *make* the reader read.

2. A TV film has a much better chance of *making* the viewer view.

Anyone who has walked into a room when the TV is on and noticed how, almost against his will, it attracts his attention, will understand what that means. The small screen grabs you despite yourself, and although you may be totally uninterested in what is going on or even skeptical about what is being shown and said, you are still, very often, forced to keep looking.

This ability of TV to make the viewer view can sometimes act as a deciding factor when you are in two minds about which of the media—press or TV—is right for a particular product. I would make the following rule-of-thumb. If the product is in a low-interest category—that means if the product has nothing intrinsically interesting about it—then probably the best medium to use, other things being equal, is television. If, on the other hand, the product is interesting in itself, then quite likely the best place to put the ad is in the press. Now I know as soon as you read that you will be able to think of half a dozen examples where exactly the opposite is the case. So let me stress, this is only a rule-of-thumb, and all other factors should be equal—which, of course, they very rarely are.

use tv for low-cost goods

There is, however, a good argument behind it. There is little or nothing of genuine interest that you can tell an audience about candy; canned fruit; pet foods; and most shampoos, deodorants, and hair sprays; they are all low-interest category products. And whenever budgets permit, their agencies promote them on TV. On the other hand, there is a great deal to be said about new cars, washing machines, stereo equipment, digital watches, and stocks and bonds, and the best ads for these products generally appear in the press. It is also worth noting that the second list— of high-interest category products—is also a list of expensive products that people buy only after a gestation period, when they mull over the different brands in their minds. So another rule-of-thumb may be surmised: The more the product costs, the less likely it is to be an appropriate subject for a TV ad.

cut your script to the bone

Let us now turn to one very basic principle in making a TV script. You would be well advised to confine your film to one main thought or promise. Even if you bought the whole commercial break, you would only have two minutes to tell your story. And you may be unlucky enough to have to cram it into one slide and 7½ seconds. The most common time length is, of course, 30 seconds. So keep your script simple. Do not, under any circumstances, prepare a lengthy and learned argument that meticulously sets out the case for your product. You simply won't have the time to put it over. Hit your audience with a single thought. And only use enough words to back up that thought in such a way as to make it believeable.

For example, commercials for Ryvita Crispbread say: "In the Inch War, Ryvita helps you win." And supporting that claim is the evidence that no matter what other kind of diet bread you buy—starch-reduced or whatever—not one has fewer calories. Then they leave it at that. They do *not* say Ryvita has a terrific taste, costs least of all crisp breads to buy, is made exclusively from natural foods, contains no additives or preservatives—nothing, in fact, except salt—comes in different varieties, and is the most popular brand in the country, selling more crispbread than all the others put together. They *could* say that, for it is all true, but in the context of a 30-second TV commercial talking to dieters, it's simply not relevant.

say something simple

This rule of only putting in your commercial a single thought may be hard for a client to swallow, especially when, as in the case of Ryvita, the product has an excellent story to tell. But you must try to make it clear to him that the average TV viewer—and we are all average TV viewers, however out-of-the-ordinary we may feel—simply won't remember more than one thought from your commercial. And this is not because he or she is stupid, but because they couldn't care less about commercials, pay very little attention to them, have a healthy skepticism toward them and expect, for the most part, only to be entertained by them. And if you want people to have a message in their minds two or three days after they have seen your spot, and when they are pushing the baby around the super-market with a million other claims attracting their attention, then say something simple.

If you do have a complicated sales message and feel—and you may be right—that you can only do justice to the product if you tell its full story all at once, then TV is no place for you. Either you go into the press, or you go on TV with what I call "cross-reference" commercials, which simply direct people to read your ad on a certain page in *TV Guide* or to write or call for your brochure, which will tell them all they need to know. If you do "cross-reference" ads, leave the address or telephone number on the screen long enough for the viewer to write it down. And remember that he probably hasn't got a pencil poised over a notepad at that particular moment.

the more pictures, the fewer words

Here is another rule-of-thumb about TV writing. If the picture is complex, the words should be minimal. If the message is complex, then the picture must be very simple. On no account should you have a fast-cutting, tension-building picture, overlaid by a wordy message. It's impossible for your audience to follow both. To give you an example: I once wrote a commercial for a glue manufacturer, in which a table was glued upside-down onto the ceiling. A rope ladder hung from the table and the idea was to have a 250-lb. man climb that ladder and sit inside the table, then throw down a weight that was attached to the table by a rope. Visible proof that the glue on the four slender legs was strong enough to carry the man and withstand the shock. Since the audience would want to see if the table was going to come unstuck, all their attention would be on the picture. So there could be no question of having a lengthy voice-over explaining how the glue was ideal for a thousand-and-one sticking jobs.

one picture, lots of words

At the other end of the scale, Cunard shipping line, when they wanted to tell people about some special reduced rates and revised sailing times for their flagship, had a commercial consisting of one shot: the QE2 sailing past a stationary camera. Five seconds looking at the picture was enough to establish all there was to see. Thus the audience could concentrate on the voice-over, and there was a good chance they could take in the various prices and dates. So remember: Dramatic pictures need little or no words. Complex messages need simple, easy-to-assimilate pictures.

steal

In previous chapters, I have had no hesitation in recommending that when you are making press ads you steal as many techniques from newspaper editors as you can. Naturally, the same advice applies when you are making a TV script. Slow motion, quick cutting (there is now a law that says you must not have cuts so short as to be subliminal), laying the soundtrack of one scene over the video of another, and all the other tricks of the film trade are constantly being refined and embellished by the top directors and film editors. The TV director of the production company you use will certainly be well up on all the latest filming devices. Unless *you* keep up with them, there can be a danger that your scripts become old-fashioned. So be aware of the movies: Be certain to see the films that innovate and, more especially, those that draw the crowds, because today's "in" film may well contain some techniques that can help you create tomorrow's "in" products.

demonstrate

The great forte of film is, of course, demonstration. I do not intend to repeat here what I have said about the tremendous value of demonstration, but let this be another rule-of-thumb for you: If you think the product will benefit by demonstration, then that is a strong argument for using TV. What kind of things can you demonstrate? You can show how the product works. You can show why it works so well. You can compare how it works alongside a rival brand. You can use cut-away models, or animation to explain sections that normally can't be seen. You can use analogies. You can dream up torture tests. You can show it in a laboratory. You can take it to the Arctic to prove it won't freeze up. The list is endless. You can also show emotional benefits, portraying how much better you'll feel about yourself when you use Brand X water softener to help clean your children's clothes.

What matters is that you provide *visible proof* your product is better. Before the viewer's eyes is conclusive evidence of your brand's superiority. Demonstrating how and why is a sure-fire way to sell. That well-known ad salesman Harry Wayne McMahan has an agency reel of 100 demonstration commercials that he is constantly updating and that, for a large fee, he will bring in and show to your creative department. If you can afford his prices, you could do a lot worse than benefit from his collection.

dialogue is more interesting than voice-over

Some people believe that the slice-of-life film is television's most effective advertising format; and certainly, if the benefits you want to put over are mainly emotional ones, then there is little to beat the playlet that can have you laughing, crying, and loving the product all in 30 seconds. There is no small skill in writing these playlets, for you need an ear for dialogue, an ability to condense that outstrips the sub-editors at *Reader's Digest*, and a keen sense of humor, as well as the talent to dream up distinctive characters. If you can do all that—and I don't think that those sorts of skills can ever be fully taught—then slice-of-life commercials can make your products, and probably yourself, famous.

name campaigns

Another great ability of TV is that, very quickly, it can make the viewer remember the name. I can only recall one press campaign that really pushed home the name of the product, and that was the Schweppes campaign, which *never mentioned the name* at all. It simply said, "You know who," and, of course, we all did know who. But on TV it is done year in, year out. The launch campaign in the UK for Tuc crackers, those little biscuits suitable for so many occasions, which were backed by a song lyric of "Tuc Tuc Tuc." And the power saw ripping through wood, steel, asbestos, plastic sheet, laminates, and the rest, with a voice pounding out "Black & Decker, Black & Decker." I even saw a motor scooter film that had teenagers zooming across the countryside to a soundtrack of "Vespa-pa-pa-pa-pa." The pa-pa-pa" being, of course, the onomatopoeic popping of the exhaust. So the technique of registering the name seems simple enough. All you have to do is say it over and over again for the length of your commercial. But nicely!

ladies and gentlemen, the presenter

Next, that good old standby, the presenter commercial. Those of you who remember the launch of commercial television will recall how we used to be subjected to presenter commercials night after night. The film would open with a fresh-faced man, sitting behind a sign saying "Marketing

Manager," who would hold up the product and gush about it until you were perfectly bemused. He'd said too much, he'd said it too quickly, he'd said it unconvincingly, and he and his ilk soon became very boring. If you thought this meant the death of the presenter commercial, you were wrong. It's just that the presenters got better, more famous, more cleverly disguised (some became cartoons, for instance), or they appeared in situations that stopped you from recognizing them as presenters at all. One film worked brilliantly, because the man started off: "Here I am in this kid's stomach . . . ," whereupon a candy the size of a tea chest fell from the roof, narrowly missing his ear. It was apposite and very funny, but it was still a presenter commercial. Later, a film opened in the middle of Death Valley with parched and cracked earth as far as the eye could see. A guy walks into the frame and explains how the dead earth has a parallel with dead skin and how a certain soap can help stop your skin dying. An incredible place, a fascinating story, an ingenious analogy, but still a presenter commercial. And finally, there is the commercial of the man who appears on the ladder of a pier, covered in the grease and gear of a cross-channel swimmer. Only he has a hamburger in his hand and starts raving—and I mean raving—about so-and-so's relish. You're fascinated, you can hardly believe it, you grin, and maybe even laugh out loud as he falls back into the ocean with one mighty splash. Highly memorable and intrusive—but a presenter commercial.

jingle jangle

And now a word about jingles. I have to admit I have never written a jingle in my life. I have also noticed that jingles go in and out of fashion and that you can have a year when the commercial breaks are filled with them followed by a year when you probably never hear one. I have no doubt that many of my readers can quote case histories by the dozen proving that jingles work. I can even remember *one* jingle, although I haven't heard it for about 20 years: "You'll wonder where the yellow went, when you brush your teeth with Pepsodent!" If you must have a jingle, I recommend that you go to the people who specialize in writing them. If you say the right thing and set it to the right kind of music, it's likely to set a number of cash register bells ringing. It's just that I can't get out of my mind that famous line about jingles:

If it's too stupid to say it, sing it.

Finally, before we close this chapter, a paragraph or two about using famous personalities. I have said most of what I want to say under the heading of WHO campaigns, but one or two points are worth reiterating. If you are going to spend a lot of money on a famous personality, you must be sure he or she is right for the product. That's probably an easy thing to decide, although you must always be prepared for the account person or client who, when you suggest a name, says: "OK, but what happens to your campaign if he dies?" If you are sure the guy is in a good state of health, has clean morals, and is not likely to get involved in a fight in a night club, then you should be certain to have a contract that says your personality won't do similar commercials for a rival product within an agreed period. And not only for a rival but, if you can afford it, for anyone at all.

stars fade if the script is faded

Having signed up your star, that is not the end of the story; you've got to write a good script. If you are dealing with a comedian, let him help provide his script with the single thought written in. If you have a beauty like Ms. Brigitte Bardot, don't think all you've got to do is let her simper; give her something sensible to say. If you use a character actor, write dialogue that *uses* his character. For example, one UK actor specializes in seeming utterly stupid. He has the face of a punch-drunk prizefighter with a voice to match, and for years he took tiny parts in feature films in which he shook a fist the size of a bunch of sausages and uttered blood-curdling threats. He then appeared in a commercial—looking immaculate. Dressed in a dinner suit, and with a perfectly dubbed voice, he spoke dialogue that was worthy of a belted Earl. The effect was both stunning and totally memorable. Here was the fool actually playing Hamlet—and UK viewers still haven't forgotten it.

If you do pay for a personality, use him or her to the full. Many's the time I have seen commercials where a half-a-dozen other characters, none of them recognizable, share the screen with the star. This is wrong, since the personality of the man—which is what you have paid so much for—rarely has the chance to come over to full effect.

Quite often, there is a tendency to hire well-known personalities to do voice-overs. Being the sort of guy who likes to get value for money, I am tempted in situations like that to preface the script with, "This is Sir Laurence Olivier speaking." If you don't say so, only one listener in a million will ever know. It's also not a bad idea, unless your hero is of international fame, to credit who he or she is.

the lure of the screen

If you are at the beginning of your career and feel that you are particularly attracted to writing for television, make a good friend of your agency TV producer and ask his advice on your ideas at an early stage. When he tells you that you can only get 60 words into a 30-second commercial, please believe him. And then write only 45 words (or less), because that is enough to have to listen to and assimilate in so short a time.

If you do make TV your forte, you may find you don't excel to the same extent in the press. Don't worry about that, at least for the first years of your business life; better to be great in one half of the media than only mediocre in both. On the other hand, you may find you are most at home writing for the press. Fine, do your utmost on paper before you try to master celluloid. The best copywriters are outstanding in both, but they are few and far between. My advice in the early stages is to go for one half of the craft and master that to the best of your ability, catching up on the other part when you know the rules and when and how to break them. But don't base your initial decision on the supposed glamor of mixing with the famous and watching the actual filming at exotic locations. In my experience, there are few things more boring than taking two days to put 30 seconds of script into a can, even if you sweated blood over every dot and comma. You can find just as much satisfaction reading your work, concisely written and properly laid out, in the pages of any paper or magazine.

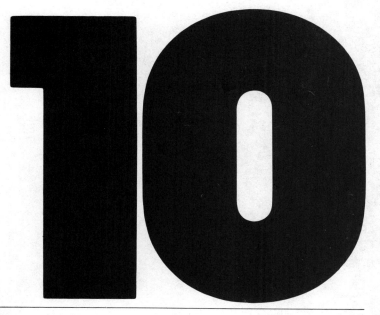

10

Talking to
the Housewife

Housewives spend most of their time in the marketplaces; creative people spend most of their working lives in comfortable offices (if you're a critic of the advertising business, you say "Ivory Towers"), and the most common accusation levied is that ne'er the twain shall meet. I shall answer the charge in good time. At the moment, however, it is enough to point out that whatever level you work at in the creative department, from director down, you will find a great deal of the advertising you make is aimed at women. And it won't take you more than a few months in an agency to realize that the products that command really large appropriations are bought mostly by housewives—cars, beer, gasoline, and oil being the only exceptions I can think of.

Because this is so, most of advertising's critics condemn the *way* we talk to housewives. Some say we caricature them and turn them into domesticated little chickens, scatter-brained sexpots, or creatures whose life is dominated by the desire first to catch, and then to keep, a man. It is claimed we talk down to women and that the inanity of some of the promises we make insults their intelligence. It's true that many of the women in TV commercials *are* caricatures. But why? Because creative people use cliché characters as a kind of shorthand to indicate the category of person the product is for. Since you have only 30 seconds to make a sales point, you can hardly build up an original and many-faceted character in your ad. So you use a cliché; and if the cliché is a home-loving little woman, at least it tells the viewer who the commercial is talking to. (Please note, I'm not excusing the practice, I'm merely explaining it.) Once in a while a really clever creative person devises a series of slice-of-life commercials where the leading lady does develop a character ("Madge" in the US Palmolive ads is a case in point). But advertising writers with the skill to create like that, and clients with the courage to buy creations like that, are few and far between.

in defense of women

Some of our critics say advertising exploits women. Talk down to, yes; deprive of helpful information, yes; insult their intelligence, yes; we do all that to women in our jobs. But I believe women have been around long enough and are tough enough and canny enough to look after themselves, and most journalists who claim otherwise are simply on the lookout for copy. One of the world's religions preaches that women, poor creatures, do not have souls, but even it concedes that they might have brains.

So how should you make ads addressed to housewives? Rule one: Give plenty of facts and all the relevant information you can lay your hands on, right down to simple things like the sizes and washing instructions. Rule two: Never make a claim you wouldn't expect a woman you know *personally* to believe. If your wife would reply, "You must be joking," to a headline, then so will everybody else's wife, unless you believe you married one of the few intelligent women in the country. Rule three: Steal techniques. I've already told you to copy newspaper editors and film directors; you should also copy the editors of women's magazines. Like everybody else in the communications business, a lot of the time they use techniques. Put this book down for a moment (if you can bear to) and pick up any women's magazine; the chances are you will find at least one item on each of the following: cookery, fashion, knitting, make-up (or hairstyles), family health, and the best way to care for your husband.

Not forgetting, of course, the obligatory love story. I don't mean this as a criticism; women's magazines simply print what most of us want to read. Here are some subjects that—if you present them with any glimmer of freshness—will never be boring.

pictures that attract

No matter how often photographers shoot them or papers and magazines print them, very few women tire of pictures of babies. No one has cashed-in on the phenomenon better than Pears Soap in the UK, who've been running their beautiful baby contest for more years than I can remember. Don't let that put you off—if you have to sell almost any product for babies, you'll have to go a long way to find many things more catchy to illustrate.

The same applies to weddings. We keep albums of our own wedding photos all our lives, and there is something about a bride and groom that will fascinate most women. Is she pretty? Is he handsome? What are they wearing? Hasn't her mother got a funny hat? The best man looks worried, doesn't he? How many commercials have you seen based on someone's wedding day? Give yours a new twist, and you're pretty sure to get attention. If babies and churches work, then put the two together and have a picture of a christening; you won't find many women who can't identify with that.

I've already said something about how journals handle fashion. It's not unknown for an advertiser selling, say, built-in kitchens, to get inquiries not about the product, but about where to buy the dress that the housewife was wearing in the ad. And finally, food pictures are always interesting, especially if the dish is new and colorful; remember the principle taught to all good cooks—we eat with our eyes.

recipes

Look in any women's magazine and you'll find a recipe. So why not use one next time you make a press ad for a food product? Research proves recipes increase readership; if anyone ever tells me they want to put one of my food ads into a starch test I always drop in a couple of recipes. Having said that, I give you a warning: Don't fool with this technique, or use it carelessly. Never accept a recipe unless, first, you have had it tried out by a qualified home economist (many big food companies have one) and, second, you have eaten the result. There is no surer way to get the housewife to hate you than to get her to make a recipe and find, after all her preparation and cooking, the meal is terrible. Moreover, there are plenty of housewives who can judge whether or not a recipe will work *before* they try it; and if what you suggest sounds stupid, they'll turn the page with a snort before you've even started to plug your bouillon cubes or whatever. What's more, you'll lay yourself open to a barrage of irate letters from disappointed ladies; and if they write to you instead of to the editor of the magazine your ad appears in, you can count yourself lucky. If any editor *does* catch you publishing lousy recipes and crucifies you for it, he's only doing his job. And trying to get you to do yours.

money-off coupons

The best time to use a coupon is when you want to persuade housewives to *try* a product for the first time. Unless this is your aim, I am skeptical about whether coupons are worthwhile. Not because housewives don't cut out coupons; of course they do. But many retailers resent those little bits of paper because they make a lot of extra work collecting and redeeming them. Not only that, but it can sometimes be very difficult for a manufacturer to ensure that his coupon is exchanged in part-payment for his product, despite what he prints to the effect that it must be so used. Some big stores will take coupons in part-exchange for anything you buy, so the only effect a coupon has is to help the housewife knock a few pennies off her final bill. Which won't do your client much good if his product remains unbought.

However, bearing in mind the casual attitude of many storekeepers and the difficulty of pinning the coupons to the goods offered, coupons still give you a few other benefits. They can help to improve the product's position on the shelf. They can encourage folk to buy a larger size of an existing product, since the coupon makes the bigger pack obviously a better value for the money. You can use coupons in specific areas, to boost a TV campaign in that same district. And since not all coupons are ever redeemed, your client can appear to the retailer to be giving away a lot more promotion money than he actually is.

As far as writing coupon ads is concerned, I think you should try to *headline* that there is money off, even though you have to say how much in the coupon. You should position the coupon on the part of the page where it can be most easily cut out, and to do that you should check with your media department whether you have a left- or right-hand page insertion. If your coupon offers very little, say a penny or two, acknowledge the fact in the body copy, not forgetting that every little bit helps. Above all, keep a sense of proportion; there are few things more laughable than the manufacturer who gives away peanuts and allows his agency to make it sound in the ads like he's offering gold blocks. If the client criticizes your copy on the grounds that you haven't made his offer sound big-deal enough, ask him how much money it would take to make his own wife rush for the scissors.

free samples

There is no stronger ad than the one that *proves* the claim it is making. And one way you can do that is to offer a free sample so the customer can put the product to the test for himself.

I once wrote a campaign for a no-calorie sweetener, where the claim was: "It leaves no after-taste." The product came in multiples of 100, but the client also made packs of only four individual sweeteners for use in restaurants. Since his production line was already geared up for these tiny quantities, I suggested that readers could send for a free sample, which was, of course, the four-pack. This is a good example of how it pays the creative person to find out all the facts about the product: It would have been quite impractical to offer a free sample if you had to give away 100 sweeteners at a time.

There is a natural instinct in account people to dismiss free samples on the grounds of expense. Always check before you leave them out of your repertoire. If a free sample proves totally impossible (and there can be many reasons apart from money), a good alternative that I think is under-used in Britain is "scratch-and-sniff." This is where a small piece of paper is impregnated with the smell of a particular product (a perfume, a new soap, a new fruit drink) and the paper is then glued in the magazine in which your ad appears. To release the smell, the reader scratches the impregnated section with a fingernail. I've always wondered why none of the men's aftershave manufacturers have used this technique, say, in ads appearing three or four weeks before Christmas. At the other end of the spectrum, a really appetizing smell could help to sell canned sauces or those foil sachets of herbs and spices that turn weekday stew into boeuf bourguignon. It's even more appropriate in these cases because you can't tell what the stuff is going to taste like until after you've bought it, while with the aftershave, at least you can ask for a sniff at the store counter.

The point about free samples and "scratch-and-sniff" is that both techniques offer you the chance to give the customer some *experience of the product*. If somebody doesn't like the way your sauce smells, you might lose a customer; but, as I never cease saying, you can't please all the people all the time.

economy sizes and value for money

This includes everything to do with making the housekeeping money go further, which is a major task of many of the women you'll be talking to. SALE advertisements should be brief and to the point. They should show the product, the old price, the new price, and the amount of money saved. Opening times of the store are vital; and if the quantity of the item on offer is limited, you must say so. No flowers of speech or arty alliterations: Give 'em the facts.

Economy sizes, if they are economy, should give the quantity and specify in cash terms how much better off the housewife is if she buys the large size. If a new package is being introduced for the first time, flash it with a money-off deal, for a limited time only. New packages are also a good place to reiterate your product story. Even old packages should be crammed with product information and offers pertaining to the product.

If what you're selling is cheap, never be afraid to say it costs less than Brand X. Some clients are squeamish about words like "cheap" and "bargain" and don't like to sell their products on a price story. Most of the time, this is nonsense. Sure, you'll probably lose the man who thinks expensive means better: He's going to buy the most expensive anyway, and very often, the more fool he. But you can also lose people who want value for money if they don't know that's what you offer. If the product is new, a price advantage can be very important indeed; if it's been around for some time, then maybe the price *flashes* on the supermarket shelf will do your good-value job for you.

If you give 20 cookies, or slices of crispbread, or spoonfuls of coffee, or ounces of jam in your package, and the competition gives less, shout it to the skies (provided always that, price-for-price, the competitive story stands up). If your kids' shoes last longer, or your trousers have two layers of material in the knee, make a big benefit of it. Best of all, give a wear guarantee. And never be scared of having a reputation for charging less than most.

If you do have to charge the most, cram your ad with information, line drawings, graphs, percentages, and beautiful, beautiful facts, which most of the time the housewife is starved of and which she badly needs if she is to convince her husband and justify to herself that the hefty price you are asking is worth paying.

As far as stretching the housekeeping money is concerned, information is what the housewife wants most, together with real efficiency and real economy. They are the keynote to selling detergents, scouring pads, air fresheners, insect killers, polishes, window cleaners—even the major purchases, such as washing machines, dishwashers, refrigerators, and vacuum cleaners. They should all be extremely efficient and not cost too much, either to buy or to run. They should be incredibly reliable, yet backed by a professional repair man. If they do break down and can't be repaired quickly, you'll never make a sale under that brand name to the same person again.

the beauty business

Cosmetics, face creams, skin-care products, dieting aids, shampoos, conditioners, hair colorants, and even hair sprays are, for the most part, sold on a minimum of information. So what happens? The buyer reads the rest of the story on the editorial pages of her favorite magazine, which is prepared to go into full details about the "dos" and "don'ts" of how to tint your hair, how long it will last, how easily it will wash out, and how much practice it takes to get it right. And if the editor tells the story, he's not going to pull any punches if your product isn't right. So, first, get it right and, second, tell the story yourself. Don't say women aren't interested: You can hook them on a new dieting aid or a new shampoo as easily as you can hook a man on a new car or a new beer.

If you have to sell any of the products listed above, remember the techniques in Chapters 6, 7, and 8. Demonstrations of how it works (for hair colorant) and how easy it is to do are meat and drink to most women. The experience of other housewives is also always good to relate; I don't think anything can beat commercials showing how women swear by their own brand of detergent, however boring we men believe them to be. Every lady, however dowdy, is interested in fashion. Ads that explain how to make a dress yourself, be certain of a perfect fit, and save money in the bargain, also have an appeal.

If you ever have to launch a new fashion, you won't go wrong if you pin it to a fashionable personality. A woman who is known for good taste and good dress sense can be a marvelous asset to your client if he wants

YOU KNOW HOW IT FEELS WHEN YOUR NAILS AREN'T RIGHT
Remember the technique of putting the product where it's least likely to work? This
is a similar technique: instead of showing what it's like when you use the product,
show what it's like when you don't. And what a nice change from all those expected
shots of beautifully manicured fingers. (Art director: *Nick Wilcox*)

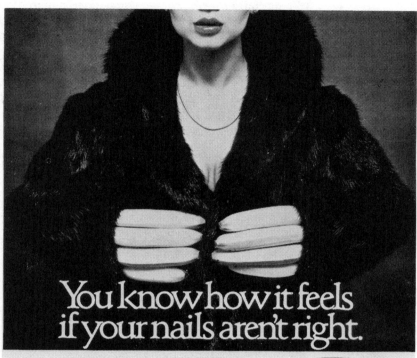

You know how it feels
if your nails aren't right.

But do you mumble the favourite excuse "I haven't got time
for fussing with nails?"

Well, now you've no excuse.

Just For Nails, from the makers of Cutipen, is the new, easy
way to nail beauty.

Each product has been carefully formulated to help get nails
looking good. And, more important, to keep them
looking good.

Short or long. With or without nail polish.

You'll find Just For Nails if you go to Boots,
larger chemists, and department stores.

And the sooner you go, the sooner you can
get your nails looking right.

All the time. JUST FOR NAILS *Cutipen*

the world to wear a new look he has created. What the First Lady wears is always interesting. What film stars wear and fashions that appear in films also have a good chance of catching on. (Remember the Great Gatsby look?) Hairstyles, too, are always good news.

The following advice may be old advice, but it's worth repeating. When you write to women, remember not to write to a category. Ask instead: Will they *believe* what you say in your advertising? Will they be interested in the way you're saying it, and have you answered all the questions likely to arise in their minds, including how much your product costs (so many advertisers nowadays leave out the price) and where to get it? I've only this minute put down a magazine with an ad promoting a new toy: It sold me on the basis of how much pleasure it would give my child, but forgot to mention how much I'd have to pay for it, where I could find it, and even omitted a manufacturer's address or phone number, killing any final hope of getting further information. These are crimes I hope no one will commit after they have read this book.

women aren't dull, so don't you be

When he was at the start of his career, the French intellectual Jean Cocteau asked what was the secret of success. "Astonish them," advised his mentor, and that's sound advice for the aspiring writer. Many of today's best-known copy and art people made their names by slaughtering sacred cows. At one time, for instance, it was death to be funny in advertising ("Nobody buys from clowns," ran the old adage). But now, as you know, viewers are disappointed if a commercial doesn't make them laugh.

Before Alka Seltzer was relaunched (in the USA), the pundits swore ads for medicines had to be straight-faced. They also swore that brand-names were sacrosanct; then somebody wrote the slogan: "With a name like Smuckers it's got to be good." For decades, agencies positioned products as the very finest of their kind; then a writer realized what a rich vein could be mined from the idea that a product that was *second* in the running had to try harder.

If you want to win yourself a reputation, *astonish*. All the guidelines are fine, but when you know and understand them, break them. For instance, when Selfridges of London needed a SALE ad but didn't want to list any of the goods in the sale, they ran a marvelous page addressed to the lines in Oxford Street. "The street-washing truck—they warned—comes round at 3 a.m." Now and again, say to yourself: I know who I'm talking to: I know what I want to say: I'm gonna say it like no one ever said it before.

The Leap
to Light Speed

Thus far, this has been a book of rules. The rules are important, for if, when learning the business, you don't work by them, then "good" and "bad" simply become a matter of opinion, and the "right" opinion is almost invariably the client's. But if you understand the rules, and more important, explain them intelligently, not only will you be respected for that understanding, but you will also ultimately be able to transcend them. And when you work from instinct, knowing not only what is right and wrong, but also knowing *why*, then you have a chance to make the leap to light speed. Let me try to describe how it works.

Back in the mid-fifties, there was an ad agency in London generally accepted as the best anywhere outside New York, and better than many inside. (Best, in this context, means it won well over the average of new business pitches, produced the most innovative and persuasive creative work, and was the agency most admired—not to say envied—by rival advertising people.) I will not name names, for, alas, how are the mighty fallen.

To maintain its considerable lead, this agency poached freely, a recruiting method common today, although much less so in London at that time. You probably know what happens: The senior directors (who have the power to hire) keep their eyes peeled for outstanding work, and when they spot it, they woo the people responsible. If the creators respond, they are offered long hours and low pay, on the understanding that the privilege of being wooed and then working for a major agency far outweighs the need to earn a salary. Sometimes the flattered creators go for it, but as often as not they ask for double what they're already earning, and so on until the right figure is reached.

After several years of wishing, I joined this agency. I'd like to pretend I had asked for double the salary, but in fact, I received a phone call from a friend who told me he was leaving and who asked if I'd like to apply for his place. Since a number of aspirants had heard of the forthcoming vacancy, competition was fierce and my own interview did not go well. But somehow we got to the question of money, and I boldly named my price. The creative director was scornful. "What do you want money for? I've not drawn a penny of my salary for the last five years?"

If I'd thought about it for a moment I'd have realized this was unlikely, probably untrue, and even impossible unless the man enjoyed a private income (or lived off his wife). But of course I didn't think about it. I simply blurted out, "Ah yes, but you're at the top!" (as if that explained anything). It was the creative director who thought about it, and his whole body began to smile. The recruiting board—there were five in all, including my friend—visibly relaxed, and I knew I'd delivered probably the best line of my (young) life. I got the job, but I had to accept the low pay.

THINK SMALL
This advertisement appeared for the first time in 1962 and still recurs in conversation among advertising people today. It stands as living proof of the one rule about creative work, which is: There are no rules about producing creative work. (Art director: *Helmut Krone*)

Think small.

Our little car isn't so much of a novelty any more.

A couple of dozen college kids don't try to squeeze inside it.

The guy at the gas station doesn't ask where the gas goes.

Nobody even stares at our shape.

In fact, some people who drive our little flivver don't even think that about 27 miles to the gallon is going any great guns.

Or using five pints of oil instead of five quarts.

Or never needing anti-freeze.

Or racking up about 40,000 miles on a set of tires.

That's because once you get used to some of our economies, you don't even think about them any more.

Except when you squeeze into a small parking spot.

Or renew your small insurance. Or pay a small repair bill. Or trade in your old VW for a new one.

Think it over.

Dealer Name

AUTHORIZED
DEALER

Happily, brilliant work wasn't expected; my task was to read and learn the rules. There actually *was* a folder of rules, which every newcomer was enjoined to grapple to his soul. Too bad for you if you didn't know the rules, or tried to break them before the right time. "Until you know the rules, don't even try to twist them" (they'd say)—a comment that only made complete sense when you noticed that the work the agency approved, and that appeared to so much acclaim, *always* broke the rules. The most senior creative people could turn them sideways, backwards, or upside down, and by doing so, double their effect. This cavalier boldness was forbidden to beginners like me; two years before the rule book being the *sine qua non* of being taken seriously.

The perceptive reader will understand that you couldn't become the best agency outside New York and make young creative people work by a book without an excellent reason. The fact is, of course, that work makes you understand the rules, and know when it's right to twist or break them. You also began to realize that all the little points add up to one big, inviolable rule: *There's a promise in every product.* The loose-leaf binder actually contained a listing of ways to coax that promise out. Not earth-shattering news—but it was treated in deadly earnest, as the following anecdote will illustrate.

Among the products of which the agency was most proud, was a dark, foamy ale, and as can happen in the best-ordered agencies, the account became loose when the creative people failed to produce a new campaign. This was, in fact, a considerable task, since the ale had nothing to say about it that drinkers didn't already know. Yet, the creative director insisted that the new campaign had to be built around a big *promise*. Three times work went to the review board, and three times he listened to how hard it had been to produce—and then rejected it. (There was no right of appeal.) Finally, the writer went back to the rule book; and sure enough, it was there in black and white. Together the creative pair chose six beautiful couples, and hired a great photographer to shoot them while they ate each other with their eyes. (The photographer's task was to make the shots memorable without making them offensive.) The art director blew up giant prints and cropped them as close as he dared. Then, over the top, they set in bold type: "There's a promise in a glass of X."

Everyone saw through it, of course, but no one could deny it made a promise. (Although many of us wondered *what* that promise was!) And here the creative director showed us why he had the job and we didn't. With a thick-nib pen he drew a small, childlike sun near the rim of every glass. At once, for no reason that I could understand, the sun took the promise away from the girl's eyes and put it back into the beer. It was a small leap to light speed.

NOW BE ANY OF THESE DELICATE BLONDES

You're not looking at a model, you're looking at a mirror. It's divided into 2″ strips, glued to cardboard, then curved toward you, with the model looking into it. Idea devised by art director Bert Steinhauser and photographer Jerry Schatzberg. The different blondes were colored in later. You can see the problem the creative team had to solve. Doing it this way was a leap to light speed. (Art director: *Bert Steinhauser*)

For nearly three years I worked to the obligatory rulebook, and never produced an ad worth a light. I spent each day in a state of creative envy, worrying about why I couldn't do it when—it seemed—everyone around me could. Finally I left, and found when I joined my new shop, that for the first time I knew what I was doing, and why I was doing it. I'd never felt so cheerful; I could look at ads pinned on my wall from the previous day and articulate why one was better than another. Everyone *knew* it was better, but few could tell a doubter why, and if you've ever tried to convince a nervy account handler that a bold proposition is also a better one, you'll know he's rarely impressed when you say, "Aw, c'mon; it just feels right."

This was not the leap to light speed, but now you're getting a sense of how many days journeying at normal speed are necessary before the quantum jump. This chapter is illustrated with ads that have made that jump, and neither I nor the people who created them will be able to explain *how* the flash came. But they will be able to tell you what's required for it to come at all.

At one of the first interviews of my life, someone told me that I either had it or I hadn't (and when anyone tells you that you can figure you haven't). When he said it, it seemed like self-evident truth and I felt low with despair. But I am living proof that the words are a simple lie, and anyone with the good fortune to work in the right place, with patient, understanding, and talented people, can create great ads in his time. Nobody is born into the copywriters' "Hall of Fame."

Where is the right place, you ask? Who are the right people? What conditions are necessary? How long must you journey at normal speed? To those questions, I can only give personal answers. So here, for the aspiring, award-hungry beginner, is all it takes to be brilliant—MAYBE!

it takes an itch

I don't know who said it, but I know it's true: If you haven't got the need, you'll never do the deed. You've got to have discontent. But first let me describe the kind of discontent you *don't* need. No matter which agency you're at, however early or late in your career, you'll meet someone who tells you what a bad place it is. The boss doesn't care; the media men are penny-pinching; the researcher is a pea-brain and the clients are sadists. Run a mile from that kind of discontent.

The kind I mean is exemplified by a best-selling author talking about how he works. No matter how he feels, he writes only *one thousand words a day*. Whether or not his creative juices are flowing makes no difference; he may revise, amend, walk away from the typewriter until after lunch, but at the end of his working hours, he's got just one thousand words. "And I even stop mid-sentence when I've reached that figure." We know this last bit is exaggeration for effect—how could he ever keep count?—but we take his point. He has discipline, he sticks to it (perhaps relies on it), writes and rewrites until his work is the best it can be—that's his discontent.

it takes a cocked ear

What are the people in your agency talking about? What's the nation talking about? Is it a war, a TV show, a society wedding, political scandal, or sports event? No matter, something is interesting them; do you know *what*? I have a colleague who likes to buy art prints. He's not an authority (other than the fact he's an art director) but he'll drop into the print shop and if he sees something he likes and he has the ready cash, it becomes his. Nothing extraordinary in that.

It's his nose that is extraordinary, because after his picture is hung, he sniffs out more about it. Where it was painted, how long it took, what art authorities say about it, where the original is kept (if that information is recorded), and so on. So when someone comes into his home and says "Gee, I like your print," he doesn't just mutter "Shucks, thanks" and tell them he likes their new suit or something.

This habit of finding out extra facts behind the subject pays off richly. Time and again I've found the ability to build just one sentence of topical information into an ad, at once spices up the sales pitch. The effect can be gained with very little effort and provided the information is one step beyond common knowledge, it can make you seem a clever and conscientious writer.

If you want an example of this practice taken to its ultimate conclusion, turn again to the Mobil "fresh killed chicken" ad in Chapter 4. When other gasoline giants were pushing extra-miles-per-gallon, offering a gram or so less lead in your gas, or putting a tiger in your tank, Mobil was stressing "We want you to live"—and was busy giving you not just the horrifying statistics of how many drivers would die that day, but also what you personally could do to improve your chances of staying alive. That's what I mean by having a cocked ear.

it takes good supervisors

There you are in the trenches, devising your sales attack, when a supervisor puts his head through the sackcloth and says he's just set a *second* team to work alongside you. "You know, fellers—just in case." *That* is a bad supervisor. Other bad supervisors are ones who won't keep you fed (overfed?) with information, who expect you to come up with the same answer they had last time, and insist you mustn't rock the boat. Or they take your completed job and never let you see (or hear of) it again.

Here is a true story of what a bad supervisor can do. Picture me reading a memo about how the agency has just been invited to pitch for a massive account. I volunteer, and the supervisor comes into my cubbyhole armed with his papers. One of the papers contains a list of fifty words, which (he explains) every user *expects* to see used about the product. How does he know? Well, someone asked them to describe the product and these are the words most used. Research shows people find *comfort* in these words. I read the list, and sure enough, they are the cliché words. And here's the punchline: Using these expected words, will I please produce an *un*expected campaign?

I try to explain that users don't actually *hear* these words anymore. Can't we devise a main thought using *un*expected words? At this point the supervisor is looking at me as though I haven't heard what he's said, and he picks up the list and stresses, very patiently, that these are *key* words.

So I produce the campaign, and it pinpoints the main thought in the strategy, which nobody will deny. However, does it use these words (they ask), and can we check how many you've managed to get in? Well, I'd managed to keep them all out—and as soon as they saw that, the campaign was dead. (Moral: If you want to live, don't be led by dunderheads.)

it helps to start at the beginning

It can happen, if you come to work on a well-established product, that the people who are connected with it have so many ideas about it that there is absolutely no room for a totally new one. So the account easiest to do great work on is often a first-time advertiser. This means there is no previously established image for it, good or bad, so that you have nothing to follow or correct, no rules to stick to, there are no taboo approaches, and unlikely to be too many sacred cows.

About sacred cows, I was once invited to work on a cigarette. The team concerned had made detailed studies of the personalities of rival brands and drawn up a profile of each. One was sophisticated, one was for people who had a sense of humor, one was for the macho type, and so on. By the time all the rivals had staked out their territories (which were expanding all the time), the only area left for my brand was "the best." The best what, you may ask, since it couldn't be the best at being witty or sophisticated or manly. Why, the best quality, of course.

LEMON
This one is a landmark, but few people know how it happened. The brief was to make an ad emphasizing VW's scrupulous inspection procedures. The writer and art director had decided to show a picture of an *apparently perfect car*, but hadn't yet hit on the right headline. A second writer (the late Rita Selden) who had nothing to do with VW, wandered into the room and said, "Why don't you just say 'Lemon'?" If only it were as easy as it sounds. (Art director: *Helmut Krone*)

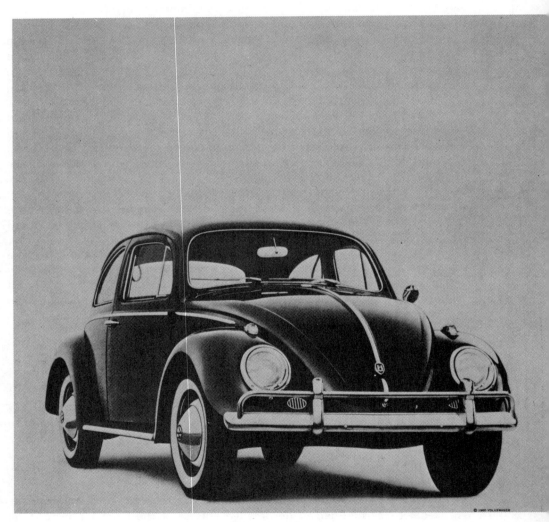

© 1960 VOLKSWAGEN

Lemon.

This Volkswagen missed the boat.

The chrome strip on the glove compartment is blemished and must be replaced. Chances are you wouldn't have noticed it; Inspector Kurt Kroner did.

There are 3,389 men at our Wolfsburg factory with only one job: to inspect Volkswagens at each stage of production. (3000 Volkswagens are produced daily; there are more inspectors than cars.)

Every shock absorber is tested (spot checking won't do), every windshield is scanned. VWs have been rejected for surface scratches barely visible to the eye.

Final inspection is really something! VW inspectors run each car off the line onto the Funktionsprüfstand (car test stand), tote up 189 check points, gun ahead to the automatic brake stand, and say "no" to one VW out of fifty.

This preoccupation with detail means the VW lasts longer and requires less maintenance, by and large, than other cars. (It also means a used VW depreciates less than any other car.)

We pluck the lemons; you get the plums.

However, I digress. Hopefully your product has something to say; examples of this are campaigns for road safety, blood donors, prevention of cruelty, and so on—where there is ample opportunity to do compelling work, not forgotting the opportunity to shock.

Hopefully, again, the appropriation you are given is a large one. While it's very nice to do conspicuous work on a small budget (and get noticed in a big way) it's even more satisfying to do the same dramatic advertising on a large budget.

It can also help if a direct competitor has done some spadework for you. I have in mind the launch of, say, a detergent into a market where only soapflakes have been available. If the competitor has already explained the basic difference between the two commodities, it means you can drop preliminaries and get on with establishing claim and brand personality.

Finally, if all those conditions exist, and you are backed by a team expecting the best, all you need is a client ready to be surprised by his advertising. Those are the ideal conditions to induce the leap to light speed. They rarely exist at the same time, so when all the forces do come together and you're invited to do the creative work, grab it.

it takes a big city

Let's say you get a skin moisturizer to write on. And since, in this example, you're a man, you know nothing about how moisturizers work. And let's say the maker tells you his product screens out harmful ultraviolet sunlight that can cause skin to age. You'll need more information, such as what doctors say, what the law allows you to say, what users believe, and whether you can lay hands on evidence (apart from that supplied by the client) to provide back-up that what you've been asked to propound is true. Not only that, but if the treatment you're introducing is a major step forward, the beauty columnists will also know of it—not to mention at least one rival. Now where, and how fast, are you going to find detailed information? Not in the sticks, but in the mainstream.

it takes authority

It is standard practice for account teams to pass to you the responsibility of producing the work, and indeed, who would have it otherwise? It is equally standard for them to deny you authority over it, once produced. Yet the big truth about good management is, no responsibility without authority.

SEED. FEED. SUCCEED.
This advertisement is a miracle of condensation. In one small page it introduces the Burpee company, establishes a whole range of seeds and fertilizers, creates an enviable image (complete with 100 year pedigree), and goes on to sell the dream of a beautiful, lavishly productive home garden. And it looks like it *just happened*. (Art director: *Rick Elkins*) Copyright 1981 W. Atlee Burpee Co., All Rights Reserved.

Clearly, there has to be a subjective judge of the work. But if you must meet deadlines, please the client, and be held responsible for results, you must also be allowed to defend work, demonstrate how style can influence content, inference can be better than statement, and less words convey more meaning. About this last, I once had to deal with a young account lady who was desperate to add as many thoughts as possible into a commercial. As her script stretched out to the crack of doom I asked her: "D'you know how many words fit into a 30-second commercial?" The thought hadn't occurred to her.

In the UK, the Creative Circle hold what they call "Role-Reversal Seminars," at which creative people become clients and clients take on the writing and art direction. These seminars run for four days, at the end of which clients have to present creative recommendations. There is no more complete way to point up the difficulties of making advertising. You soon get tired of the surprised complaint: "I never knew it could be so hard."

so what does it take to be brilliant?

Most of all, of course, it takes luck. If you're accepted into a skilled agency, helped by high-caliber people, and deal with clients and account handlers who expect and admire the best, what else is that but luck? I know creative people who could enjoy an easier life, a more impressive title, and a bigger paycheck elsewhere, but who eschew these blandishments in order to enjoy that luck.

It takes a driving ambition (the itch, remember). It takes a long time traveling at normal speed (no infants in the Hall of Fame). It takes an ability to stop kidding yourself that your best ads ended up in the wastepaper basket, when in fact they're the ads that ran. (The others are nowhere.) It takes good officers and more brave men in the field than you. When William Shakespeare wrote his plays he had a choice of great actors, skilled musicians and costume designers, a keen and educated audience, patronage, was in favor in the Royal House, and built his own theatre. Without those things, no plays.

It helps to start with a clean sheet and a large budget. It takes a big city and easy access to information and other services. It takes a good teammate, authority, time, and last and most important, bristling antennae and genuine *thought*. How can you tell whether you've finally got it right? Believe me, you'll *know*. But to articulate the reasons, read the next chapter.

How to Judge
Your Work

In a sense, this is probably the most important chapter in the book. I am going to list seven criteria you can use to decide whether you have made a good ad. But a moment's thought will show you that this is not simply a checklist; it sets a standard to which all your work should aspire. I call these criteria the seven silver rules for judging creative work: silver rules, because there is only one golden rule, and that is, "There are no rules when you create advertising." If you apply these rules—as and when they are appropriate—you will become a good copywriter. If you ignore them, or feel that some are too harsh to apply, then you'll always find someone saying "could do better."

But first a word of encouragement to the trainee who reads the list and feels he's never going to be able to make ads that live up to it. Don't forget you are learning your craft; nobody expects you to be brilliant after only a year or so at your desk. Like the author, playwright, or scriptwriter, you will only become proficient through practice. If I have learned one thing in our business it is "the less you do, the less you want to do." And if you sit around in your agency sidestepping jobs, you will soon find you have lost the inclination to make any ads at all. *So be hungry for work.* Nobody in any office is busy all the time; if, during one of those lulls, someone asks if you're interested in taking a brief to help out a colleague, grab the chance. Even if it's only to do a run-of-the-mill trade ad, there are still countless ways trade ads can be done differently, and it is a chance to practice. Your creative director and the account people will soon recognize a willing worker. You will be given bigger and better chances. When you get briefed to make an ad today, it might take you a long time to assimilate the facts and produce an idea; persist, apply the seven silver rules, and before too long you will be able to field anything anyone throws at you.

the urgent copy date

The biggest problem most young creative people have is dealing with deadlines; it is a fact of life that advertising is geared to copy dates, and you will find that often you are asked to work very fast. The agency management should have impressed on the account people the importance of giving you as much time as possible; if one particular account person makes a habit of bringing you panic jobs, the best thing to do is ask your creative director to put matters right. But, I must emphasize, there is no profit in worry. (I once met a guy who believed he was paid to worry. What nonsense. He was actually paid to keep a level head and stop other people from worrying.) You will never produce your best work if you are uptight with worries and tensions. The more relaxed you are, the better your brain will work. It is because I understand how easy it is to worry over deadlines that I have described in such detail the *practical steps* that will lead you to ideas.

Feeding your mind with facts about the product, the customer, and the medium you're going to use is like fertilizing soil. When you've got enough information to work on, solutions begin to grow almost automatically. The best antidote for worry is to busy yourself finding out all you can about what you have to sell. When it comes to making ads, there is no substitute for application.

But enough of this preaching, let's get to the seven silver rules. You remember how I told you it was a good idea, when you had made one or two ads, to pin them to your office wall and give them the "overnight" test? Well, when you come into the office fresh next morning, here are the seven questions to ask:

1. *Is it "on strategy?"* You might think this criterion is so obvious as to be not worth mentioning: You'd be surprised. You see, sometimes when creative people are at work, they come up with a brilliant solution—except that it's not in line with the strategy. Never mind, they think, this idea is so good that we might persuade the client to buy it despite the fact that it's not what we planned to say.

Ninety-nine times out of a hundred, when this happens, the creative team are being propelled by their own (quite natural) enthusiasm; a brilliant idea is only brilliant if it's saying the right things. This is not to say that there has never been an occasion when an outstanding creative solution has brought about a revision of the strategy; far from it. But you must be careful, before you go back to change basic thinking, that you're doing it for the right reasons.

Most strategies should be written so they isolate the main thought the advertising campaign has to communicate. (Turn back to Chapter 5 for a reminder of how strategies are composed.) What you have to ask is whether your ad has hit the main thought firmly on the head and put it over in the tone of voice that the customer likes to hear. If you will answer "yes" to that question, then your work is "on strategy."

2. *Is it clear who you're talking to?* By now you're probably tired of reading the question, *who are you talking to?* But if you only remember one thing from the whole of this book, that is the one most worth remembering. There isn't a newspaper or magazine editor, a playwright, an author, a film director, or a composer who doesn't know who his audience is. They all

decide, first and foremost, who they are writing for, and note this—none of them tries to write for everyone.

You know who's going to buy *Sports Illustrated*; you know the audience *Reader's Digest* reaches; you certainly know who *Ms. Magazine* is for. *The New York Post* never writes editorials to impress readers of *The New York Times*. The best feature-film director in the world never tries to please everyone. The man who composes a pop tune writes for a different world than the man who composes a violin concerto. Every one of them knows that if you try to reach everyone, you get no one. It is vitally important that you make this clear to your clients, who understandably feel that the bigger audience they reach, the more goods they will sell. It isn't so.

> *If a feature film can't please everybody, if a novel can't please every-body, if music by a great composer can't please everybody, how can one ad please everybody?*

My first boss put it at its most basic: "If you're selling wooden legs, the headline's gotta be: "To all one-legged men." Well, I don't entirely agree, but the principle is right. There is a school of thought that says if you're talking to young men, show young men in the picture; if you're talking to older women, show older women; mothers, show mothers; brick-layers, show brick-layers, and so on. If you're not certain of the kind of person to illustrate, it's a good rule-of-thumb, though I can't promise it will make you devastating ads.

3. *Is your ad interesting?* Think about it; can you really expect anyone to be interested in a dull ad? Is the piece of work you pinned to your wall telling the reader something he doesn't know? Does it look like it's going to inform? Or be fun to read? Is it the kind of ad that will draw you deep into the body copy? Is it going to keep you going as long as it keeps going? Does it offer a clear reward for reading? The questions are so logical, yet it's perfectly obvious from work that appears every day in the press (and on TV) that not many creative people ever ask them.

Some products are actually dull products. I've explained what to do then—use showmanship. One thing you can be sure of; if you find the ad boring to make, the world will find it boring to read (or watch). The only way to get an audience enthusiastic is to be enthusiastic yourself. Nothing irritates me more than to see creative people tackle an ad with an "Oh God, I suppose I've got to do this" attitude.

And it's no good putting up the excuse that although most people find a subject uninteresting, there are a few who are fascinated by the product and that it's only them you're trying to reach. Some people do plough through ads despite the creative teams' efforts, but that's no credit to the copywriter. Remember this: As far as creative people are concerned, there should be no boring products, no dull companies, and no unimaginative sales pitches—only dull, boring, unimaginative advertising.

4. *Is your ad instant?* The average ad has about 1½ seconds to say, "We've got something for you!" That's how long the reader pauses over it, considering whether it's worth his while to read on. We can learn a lot from this. First, if the promise you are making hasn't come across in that 1½ seconds, then it'll never get across. Nobody reads on into the body text of an ad if they haven't grasped the proposition in the headline and picture. (Yes, I know you can capture attention with trick and shocker headlines, but they almost invariably let the reader down when he reads on to find what they're about.)

It's good policy, therefore, to look on your press ads as posters. You know a poster has to make sense without any body copy; ideally a press ad should stand up to this test too. Body text in a press ad is to back up your main thought with relevant facts. You try to arouse a wish in the reader to own the product. Then you convince him that he'll benefit greatly and that any money he spends will be a wise investment. Then you tell him what to do (visit the showroom, fill in the coupon, call this number now). But the big promise has to sing out straightaway. I would like a dollar in my pocket for every time I heard a creative team justifying an oblique headline by saying, "Ah, they'll understand as soon as they read on!"

5. *Is your ad believable?* Sometimes creative people can be very strange. They can write down a piece of nonsense on a layout pad, and, because it rhymes or has a neat beat to it, they think the style—plus the fact that it will shortly appear in print—will make it incontrovertible. Yet if you took those very same words and *spoke* them to the creative man concerned, he'd scratch his head and tell you not to be so silly. Some copywriters can put dialogue into the mouths of characters in commercials that would not be out of place in a lunatic asylum. Let me quote an example. (This is not to take a knock at the advertiser concerned, or indeed the creative people concerned; it's simply taken from memory at random to show you exactly what happens.) A television campaign that has been running in the UK for some years is based on the line: "Mellow Birds will make you smile." Birds is the name of the manufacturer, the product is an instant coffee, and the product claim is that the granules produce a more mellow drink than other instant brands. (The claim is too stupid to say, so they sing it.) But

if you walked up to the copywriter who wrote that line, with a jar of the product, and said to him, "This coffee will make you smile," he'd say: "Why? What's funny about it?" Bird's Mellow Coffee will please, possibly. It might win compliments for its new taste. It might lead someone to ask for a second cup. It might get you a name as a discerning coffee drinker. But there's one thing not even the finest Jamaican Blue Mountain coffee has ever done to me, and that is make me smile.

What happened is that the creative team got into their office that morning, shut the door, and disappeared down a secret tunnel into Adland. And in Adland people go around in ecstasy at the mention of the product name. They believe promises that a child of five would think preposterous. And they talk a language peppered with words like exciting, unique, greatest, and best-in-the-world. Now I know you, dear reader, are not among that type of creative person; you are quick-witted and intelligent (or you wouldn't be reading this book). But I mention the existence of Adland to make certain that you never go there, for it is a crazy place where people will believe anything, despite the fact that it is transparent nonsense. Make your work believable; don't *kid* yourself that you believe it or that other people who are not so discerning as you will believe it. Ask yourself: Is this genuinely credible?

6. *Is your ad unexpected?* Is that question unexpected? Then maybe you have always made ads the expected way, when being unexpected can increase the impact of your work tenfold. Since it is your job to make ads, you probably spend a great deal of time reading ads made by others. Have you noticed how there are some ads you instinctively avoid because *you know what they are going to say?* You can repeat the promises offhand; the copywriter can start a sentence and you can finish it for him. The most obvious example is cigarette advertising, where copywriters are reduced to a 20-word vocabulary (taste, value, flavor, best, finest Virginia—add the rest yourself, there aren't that many). An unexpected interpretation of a selling claim can make a $250,000 appropriation feel like a $1,250,000 appropriation.

Here is something I have discovered about how to produce unexpected ads. First, you go through the usual process—learning about the product, the market, and the media. Then you make your ads; you work hard at them and put them on the wall for the "overnight test." Then you forget about them for maybe three or four days. Sometimes it's quite a good idea to turn to a different job altogether, just letting the main thoughts of the ads on your wall rest under the surface of your mind. (Don't worry over it or dig it up to look at it; leave it there and let your subconscious work on it for as long as you have time available.) If you're lucky, when you come back to your work, a quite remarkable thing can happen; the unconscious thinking you've been doing can suddenly show you a completely new way to make the ad. Your brain has been at work without any direct help from you; all you did was feed it the facts, produce a few expected ads, and let those efforts lie under the surface of the mind.

This "seeing with new eyes" can also happen if you've taken the trouble to write body copy for your ads. Re-reading it, you may well find that about three-quarters of the way through there's a phrase or sentence that throws quite a different light on what you're trying to say. You can put this to the test now; pick up any newspaper you like and read through half-a-dozen quite ordinary ads. I'm prepared to wager that down in the body copy, where few people go, there's a line that—if it had been spotted— could have brought the ad to life. I understand that one reason why this line so often remains unused is that the creative people are so pressed for time that they haven't a chance to let the work lie for a "gestation" period. It's worth telling people who ask you to work at express speed that in the end they only get the advertising they deserve.

7. *Has your ad proved its case?*   Proving an argument isn't just the best way to make a sale; it's also probably the most difficult thing any ad can do. There are plenty of cases, of course, where a claim can't be proved. *Beanz Meanz Heinz. Happiness is egg-shaped. Central heating for kids.* How do you go about providing proof for slogans like these? But a great number of claims can be proved. When London's Metropolitan Police set out to recruit for the force, they proved that a policeman's life was more interesting, responsible, and rewarding than almost any job offering a comparable income (and many paying a lot less).

When the UK Government ran ads to recruit nurses, they proved a nurse was a girl you would trust with your life, a girl whose opinion was valued even by hospital consultants, and a girl whose contribution to an operation could be crucial. Another ad, which invited readers to place their fingers on the headlights of a car, proved how easy it was to be unseen in fog (when the lamps disappeared, so did the vehicle).

If you are looking for ways to prove your claims, seek out people who can give independent advice. Your readers know that if the manufacturer says something, he's saying it because he wants you to buy his product— and what's more, he doesn't mind exaggerating a bit to make a point. But when an independent scientist, or a sports car reporter, or a satisfied user, or *Consumer Reports* magazine says something, it isn't the manufacturer talking, and you have a much better chance of being believed. Bloggs Brand isn't best because Mr. Bloggs says so. But if Mr. Bloggs' chief competitor admits that old Bloggs doesn't make such a bad product, that's real reason to buy.

So there are the seven silver rules to apply when you are assessing your work. If a new ad or campaign meets all the criteria, then you should have a block-buster that breaks every sales record in the book (remembering always that the quickest way to kill a bad product is with outstanding advertising). One more piece of advice. It wouldn't be a bad idea if you made this checklist public; in other words, showed the account people you work for how you assess an ad before you hand it over to them. Since very few people have any idea at all about how to assess creative work, the fact that you have a pretty rigorous system should carry some weight. If they know that the work they take to clients complies with these silver rules, they can use the knowledge to help sell the work, because the rules show that the work isn't top-of-the-head stuff but has been produced by craftsmen working under a discipline. The rules make sure the ads are saying the right things to the right people in the right way, and what client will turn down work that can promise all that?

How to Defend Your Artwork

When you decide to become a creative person in advertising (and there are few more interesting jobs), you have to recognize that probably two-thirds of the work you do is never going to appear. The very nature of the job means that every ad you make has a great many hurdles to jump before it gets presented to a client, and then, very often, your troubles are just beginning. A very talented art director once told me that if he managed to end his working year with three campaigns, either in print or on film, he counted himself lucky. Three campaigns a year may not seem many if you are a young enthusiastic writer ready to work till all hours to build up experience. But after 25 years in the business, the work that I have to show, including campaigns that I have now discarded because they are dated, amounts to considerably less than that. So you may as well learn to accept, as early as you can, that even ads that you consider to be among the best you have ever made will, as often as not, remain forever in layout form. If you can keep that thought in mind, and if you can also be careful to cultivate a sense of proportion (by which I mean that although making ads is your work, they are, after all, only ads), you will have a happier working life than if you expect anything you do to sail through the system unopposed.

Let us look for a moment at the hurdles your ads will encounter in their journey to the public eye. The very sternest critic you will ever have to deal with should be yourself. A first thought may indeed prove to be a best thought, but do not be content with it from the outset. Cross-check that the ad says with crystal clarity who it is talking to.

showing work to your boss

Be certain you are saying exactly what you want to say and saying it in the right tone of voice. If your ad comes up to scratch on these criteria, then try it on your creative director.

Remember, it is his job, his *raison d'etre* almost, to maintain creative standards in the agency, so he will probably be the second-sternest critic of your work. You must hope that he is judging it from a background of knowledge (a gut-feel if you like) of whether it will do the job for which it is intended. If he says "no," don't throw a tantrum or drop into the pit of despair; sound him out as to how he thinks it can be improved, and if you don't take every word he says as gospel, at least give his suggestions a fair hearing. Remember that if he says "yes," then it goes to the account people (the next hurdle) with all his authority behind it; the responsibility for its efficacy has moved from you to him. The account people will bombard you with all the doubt they think the client may have. Yes, they are second-guessing his reaction, but remember again that they are the guys who took the initial *brief* and be patient if they voice suggestions as to how your work might be improved. Please don't fight for every period and comma in the draft copy. Rarely has any piece of copy that I have written passed through the system totally unscathed.

The next stop is the review board, which is generally held whenever there is a major new batch of work going through the agency. For a review board, you should muster all your facts and have a full knowledge of the product and the customer ready at your fingertips. Very often you can be made to look foolish if someone pops up in the review board with a set of figures or an attitude unearthed by research of which you were not aware. (Not that this should ever happen, since it is the account people's *duty* to be certain that every relevant piece of information has reached your office, even before you put pen to layout pad.) If your work goes through the review board, it means that the whole agency has put its authority behind it. This is a point that account people should bear in mind during the client presentation; whatever the client says, a body of highly experienced advertising people has studied the work, and in their opinion it is doing exactly what the marketplace calls for, in the best way they can imagine.

meeting the man who pays the bills

By now you are ready to meet the client; you have been through all the questions he could ask and presumably you have good answers to them. In client meetings, you should be wary of any show of irritation or impatience. Your work will stand a much better chance of being accepted if the client sees you not just as a creative person but as a responsible business person who understands his problems, and acknowledges that you are spending *his* money. If he can look on you as a friend as well as a business associate, you will have a much better relationship than if he learns to see you as a protagonist. You will never win a war against a client, because in the last analysis he has the right to say "no" to a campaign; he pays for that right by contributing to your salary.

One question the wise creative person asks himself when he comes up against fair opposition in a client meeting is: "If it were my money that were being spent on this advertisement, would I still go ahead and spend it?" That's a sobering thought and one that will bring any sensible creative man down from a pitch of indignation when the client queries whether a particular phrase used to express a sales point is quite as clear as it might be.

You will probably find that the client is several people, and you will not always have a chance to sell your ad to them all at the same meeting. The lower ranks of the client's hierarchy are often the toughest to get through, since (unhappily) they may also be second-guessing and want to pre-empt their boss's comments by making them themselves. Patience and logic are your weapons now; never throw them away in favor of temperament. The final OK may rest with someone as high up as the managing director. It is not his job to be able to tell good ads from bad ads; it's your job. But that doesn't give you the right to say "I'm the professional—you've got to accept my word." Quite the opposite; you've got to be logical enough and articulate enough to *prove* that your work is right. If every managing director could distinguish good from bad, there wouldn't be any bad ads around. No one, either inside or outside our business, would deny that today bad ads actually predominate.

I hope these last pages have helped explain why three campaigns a year is an acceptable success rate. And although I have tried to stress that level-headedness is the best help in selling campaigns, I do not intend that you should present your work with a mouse-like timidity—not that I've ever met a mouse-like creative person. I could fill a book triple this size with criticisms you might meet in your working life and still not have covered half of them. But since there are some that constantly crop up— and have no substance when looked at in the light of common sense—I list them below, with some arguments to refute them.

what if you run it without the sound?

This is a trick the old-hand account person will sometimes try to pull on you when he is judging your TV storyboard. He looks at the pictures to see what is being shown; he reads the words to see what is being said; then he asks if anyone will understand the commercial if you turn off the sound. I don't know how this criterion was first arrived at; I suspect it came into being when someone realized not everyone gives 100 percent of their attention to commercials. Then they said to themselves: "If we show the same thing as we tell, we'll capture more customers." There are three ways to counter this argument:

1. A stand-up comic, the world's greatest opera singer, and a fine musician are all dead if you turn off the sound. All the subtleties of humor, tone of voice, nuances that suggest product benefits, the

additional qualities that music and laughter can give your commercial are lost by asking if it works in silence.

2. Anyone not giving their attention to what is being *said* in a commercial is almost certainly also not giving their attention to what is being *shown*; so you've lost them anyway. Although TV companies may charge you for every set switched on at any time, you will never get everyone in front of a TV to give you their undivided attention all the time.

3. The simple fact of life is that viewers *don't* turn off the sound. And some of the best commercials gain their force from a juxtaposition between words and pictures. I would say that any commercial that can be understood completely with the sound off is only half a commercial and should be rejected on that criterion, rather than be found acceptable on it.

nobody reads body copy

You've got to be careful of this one, because if your message doesn't come over after people have seen the headline and the pictures, you've got a bad ad, so it's no good saying they'll understand when they read the body copy. That's when it's quite true that nobody reads body copy. But if your picture and headline tell the story (or part of it) and you then expand on the benefits, you are on sounder ground.

Nobody reads *bad* body copy; that is, copy that waffles, lacks facts, is badly constructed, and gives no reward for reading. But people do read good copy. Say you are doing an agency house ad (and those are very often the hardest to make), and you write a headline: "How to spot a *bad* advertising agency." If there is room under that line for hundreds of words, anyone on the lookout for a good agency will almost certainly continue to read the ad so long as it tells him things he doesn't know.

The question, "How long should an advertisement be?" is the same question as "How long is a piece of string?" There is no *rule*. An ad is too short if it ends without saying the right things to make a sale. An ad is too long if it repeats itself, gets boring, stops giving facts and information, or uses two words when one would do. If you want a guideline on how to judge what the right length of any headline, baseline, or piece of copy should be, then consider its *content*. If that is right, the length isn't often wrong.

mrs. bloggs won't get it

This criticism is very common. You show an account person your ad, he smiles, nods sagely, rubs his chin for a couple of seconds, and says: "Ah, I get it, but will the average housewife in Peoria?" implying that, as an intelligent and highly paid ad-man, he is *au fait* with the nuances and sophistications of the big city, but that dull old housewives, west of the Mississippi, are totally mystified by any novel, stage play, or radio or TV show that rises above street level. And consequently, your ad must appeal to the lowest common denominator or it is a dead duck. The common result of a criticism like this is that you produce ads that ignore intelligent people, thereby encouraging intelligent people to ignore your ads. There is a common belief in our business that the majority of the population are idiots. I hope you will have gathered enough from this book to know that I refute the belief and state that, on the contrary, almost everyone in the world knows something you don't and that advertisements should, if anything, write *up* to people rather than talk down to them. But note well: This is *not* an excuse for writing ads that Mrs. Bloggs genuinely won't understand.

any product could say that!

There is a slogan in the UK, "Go to work on an egg." But the copywriter could just as easily have said "bacon sandwich" or "bread and cheese" or "Quaker Oats."

The fact is, eggs said it first, so anyone who says it second is simply helping to remind people of the original slogan. The same applies to The Inch War. It was said for Ryvita, but it could equally well apply to any dieting product. The simple fact is, a product without a unique selling proposition can have a unique selling *personality*. So, as a creative person, you have to decide whether there is something unique and relevant you can say about your product; if there isn't, then go for a generic campaign and do not knuckle under to an unthinking critic. If he persists and refuses to admit that scores of products are using slogans that could equally well have been used by their competitors *provided they had thought of them first*, then you will have to ask him outright to define the USP for you. If he does it, you're wrong; but if he can't, then he should shut up and be glad that you have created a personality that the client can make his own.

our competitor uses that word!

This criticism is really sneaky because it implies that the creative people have been stealing someone else's work. But it is still commonplace. Your client makes beautiful furniture, and you say so. Then you come across an ad for A. Smith that says his furniture is beautiful. Oh dear, you can't use the word beautiful because Smith's have already used it. They've also used lovely, attractive, pretty, appealing, and desirable, so you can cross out all those words too. The only guy who should be pleased about that is Smith, because you have, at a stroke, granted him a monopoly on all those words and gagged yourself into the bargain. The rule here is simple to follow; if you are making the same claim as your competitor, then that's the time to rethink. But if the sense of what you are saying is quite different, then it matters not one jot, and indeed it might even be inevitable that you use some of the same words. I would add that you should apply common sense, but very often when ads are being judged, common sense is in very short supply.

don't say it isn't so;
they might think it is

This is really a Catch 22 situation. Say you are advertising a book club. Now the problem with book clubs is that people think they will be under the obligation to buy a lot of books. So the writer puts in a clause about "no obligation." Ah, says the account person, mentioning that there is no obligation will make people think there *is* one. Or again, your ad carries a coupon that assures readers that if they fill it in, they will get literature, but no one will call. Ah, they say, isn't that suggesting that someone *will* call? Or again, you put in a clause that promises money back if not satisfied. Ah, isn't that suggesting they might *not* be satisfied? Well, actually, no. Not unless you believe that if the ad says, "available in white," people will actually believe the product is available in black. Words mean what they say, and if a customer feels he may be under an obligation, or that someone will call, or that he may not be happy with whatever he has bought, it's only sane to reassure him. I think the only riposte to comments like that is to ask the offender whether he believes that if you say the product is good, people will actually believe it's bad. And when he says "yes" (which he will), then ask him why he is advertising at all.

you should never ask
a question in a headline

The only answer to this nonsense is to find a really terrific ad that has a question as a headline, stick it down on a large piece of layout paper, and headline it: "Why is this ad wrong?"

it's not a women's magazine ad

I once made a campaign for a product bought by women. The obvious medium for it was the women's magazines. But the art director, clever fellow, made the ads very graphic; the photographs were brilliantly simple, the type was beautifully set, and the visuals, finished off with acetate, looked as though they had come out of *Vogue* magazine.

We presented them to the client. He fell for the proposition right away and thought we had done a marvelous job interpreting the strategy. But, he went on, they don't look like women's magazine ads; they look like they came out of *Vogue*. Can't you make them more in keeping with the medium they'll appear in? Now pause there, dear reader, because you are in a very dangerous position of making the client look a fool, which is not a wise thing to do. So, in the most delicate way possible, you have to ask him whether the ads, when they appear in *Family Circle* and *Good House-keeping*, will stick out like a sore thumb. And when he says, "Yes," say, "Good."

And now a few words about some criticisms you *should* pay attention to.

it's ad-y

That could mean your advertisement looks like an advertisement, sounds like an advertisement, and is in every way just what people expect an advertisement to be. Can this be bad? Yes, because people are inclined to disbelieve advertisements and to ignore every piece of print that looks like an advertisement. So the criticism, "it's ad-y" is a non-cliché way of saying that your whole ad is a cliché. Strange though it may seem, ads that don't look like ads can be a very effective way to get attention.

There was once a technique, used very well by the Milk Marketing Board, of making ads that looked like the beginning of a piece of fiction.

They contained the same kind of illustrations and the same typography that the women's magazines used to present love stories. And, of course, they appeared in women's magazines. This technique is now expressly forbidden (more-the-pity, since magazines have become duller for it), but you can see the principle. Making an ad look like a part of the editorial, provided it is done intelligently, can increase initial readership. Ad-y-ness is when you persist in using tired old phrases and hackneyed similes to promote your product when impact could be trebled and interest revitalized with a new idea. Expressing an old proposition with new words gets it seen with new eyes and sets the mind to work considering it. It's the key to advertising "creativity" and the frequency with which you are able to do it will decide whether you become a respected copywriter or not. Please steer clear of the clichés and *déjà vu* graphics that are the stock-in-trade of the advertising hack. They do neither you nor the advertising business any good at all.

it's expected

This is a very similar criticism to the last, but I include it because some creative people are surprised that their work should strive to be unexpected. They think, for example, that a perfume ad isn't a perfume ad unless it looks like a perfume ad. The real craftsmen know that unexpectedness is part of making ads; they will go to extremes to find a new angle on an old promise. And that doesn't mean just finding new words to express an old thought. "It'll help you get your man" is not the only thing you can say about perfume, just as "It'll help you get your woman" is about the most boring thing you can say about aftershave lotion. So once you know who you are talking to, don't just plump for the thing you think they want to hear.

I was once given the job of promoting a fizzy drink, made, as it happens, with real fruit. Not much real fruit, but at least more than you get in Coke or Pepsi. The account people wanted me to promote the theme, "made with real fruit" (surprise, surprise), but not only was the claim boring, there was so little real fruit in the fizz that it was totally unbelievable. Instead, I suggested a campaign to persuade mothers to include a can of the drink in their kid's lunchboxes every morning. In Britain, free school milk had just been discontinued, and the kids were looking for something to sip in the morning recess. So instead of commercials shouting, "Drink Pop, it's made with real fruit," we ran ads saying, "Put a little bit of fruit in his lunchbox" and "A little bit of fruit helps restore pupil power!" You don't ignore the obvious claim; you just try to make it unexpected.

it's boring

In all my time in the business, I haven't yet found an answer to this one. It's the hardest of all criticisms to answer (yet surprisingly, it's one that is rarely levied at you by account people). They will often buy an ad that could send a reader to sleep on a bed of nails, provided they think it's "the right message." But very often the obviously right message is wrong because it is so obvious.

I think the best way to decide whether or not an ad is boring is to ask yourself: "Would I read it?" That may not seem to be saying much at first glance, but think back to what I said about subjects that are intrinsically interesting (cars, entertainment, drunkenness, contraception, road safety, careers) and products that are uninteresting (soaps, baked beans, steam-baked bread, canned fruit, ice cream, chocolates). If there is nothing you can say that is unexpected about the product, remember the rule: showmanship! Get some interest from somewhere, even if it's only spectacle. (I once saw a medicine for stomach upsets sold by dressing actors up as gherkins, peppers, onions, rich cheese, and some of the other foods that are delicious to eat but upsetting afterwards.) Sometimes you may be attacked for using what is called "borrowed interest," but if a product is totally uninteresting, and plenty are, then even "borrowed interest" is better than no interest at all.

In the last analysis, you know yourself whether an ad is boring; if you are, as I recommend, your own sternest critic, you will decide, however weary you feel, that it's worth one last try. I know it's easy to say "boring," but when you look at the number of ads around that really *are*, don't you wish some creative people tried harder?

I will end with a warning. There really is nothing more tedious than a creative team defending an ad that isn't worth the paper it's written on. I have seen it many times, and as the tempers rise and the language degenerates, do try to remember, if you are an account person, that rash defenses are often born of insecurity. A creative person has willingly put himself in the engine room of the agency, and there can be times when he can't have an idea at any price. I counsel firmness but kindness. And to creative people who see their best work end up in the wastepaper basket, there are two things you can do. Rescue some of it and take it to a creative director you respect. If he offers you a job, take it, because you are in the wrong agency, and your talent is being wasted. If you don't want to move but still can't get your ads through the system, remember that they are only ads. And read Chapter 14.

How to Present
Your Artwork

I believe in one basic rule in presenting creative work to clients: The presentation should be made by the people who did the work. This may not always be possible. Sometimes the people who made the ads might not want to present them. Sometimes they are so slow on their feet that it takes a more nimble tongue and quicker wit to "sell" the work to a client. Sometimes it may be agency policy to divorce the creative department completely from the client. There are two reasons for this: First, the creative people may be so close to the work that they cannot acknowledge it has any defects at all, so they tend to become aggressive if the meeting does not go well. Second, there may be times when a client gets attached to a creative team, which can be embarrassing for an agency if that team decides to go elsewhere: The client may decide he wants to follow them. There is one very successful agency in London where the creative people never present the work, yet some might say the same agency owns some of the most talented created people around. Notwithstanding the exceptions, I stick by my first assertion. If you made the ad, then you should present it.

Why? Because when you made the ad you learned all about the product and all about the customers, so you know exactly why you did it the way you did and can explain those reasons at the meeting. But more important, you have got to face the man whose money you are spending and defend your work. If you haven't done your best, then you will have to take the flak for it. You can't hide behind some hapless executive while the client pounds him for missing some of the best selling features of his product. Moreover, since you are originators, you are also very committed to your work and consequently should be able to put it in its best light. Finally, if the work is turned down, you will know why it was turned down and how it was turned down, and you will have no one to blame for the rejection but yourself.

This is not to say I think that account people don't put their hearts into selling good work. Far from it. I once worked with a very senior account person who, if he was happy with a campaign and convinced it would do its job, would go to the wall to defend it. He took stands at meetings at which I was present that were far more extreme than I would have taken myself. Where I would have compromised, he was adamant, and nine times out of ten he got away with it. Certainly, it was a pleasure to work for him, since his firm commitment made it incumbent on me to turn out the very best possible job.

use your main advantage

Whenever you walk into a client presentation you should remember that, until the campaign has been shown, you are in a highly advantageous position. There is no time in the client–agency relationship when you have so much of the client's rapt and undivided attention. He wants to see the creative work, he wants to be surprised, he hopes he will also be convinced the ads are right, and he is looking forward to advertisements that excite him. Moreover you are talking about the one subject most dear to him—the product he has spent his career making and selling.

All the time he is listening to the preamble, he is thinking about the work. Charts are nice, media plans are nice, research findings can be fascinating; but nothing is more "grabby" than actually being introduced to the theme of a new campaign and being shown how it develops into a series of advertisements, each building on a different aspect of the product, or presenting the proposition in a slightly different way to emphasize one feature, then another, until the whole product personality has evolved. At this time, you should have the client in the palm of your hand, and he will look at your layouts, race ahead of you to read your headlines and assimilate your argument for the product, and only in exceptional circumstances interrupt the flow of your presentation.

first impressions matter

There is a lot to be learned from this simple fact. First, your advertisements should look good. I'm not suggesting that you typeset headlines, take experimental photographs, and cover the lot with acetate and glossy masking paper. Very often these refinements are used to disguise the fact that the work is poor.

But I am suggesting that if you have a good idea, see that the presentation does it justice. Regardless of how many times clients tell you they can "read" roughs, or that they only want to see your basic thoughts you simply cannot produce basic thoughts in a client presentation; you have to come up with the final concept: Otherwise it's back to square one, and you're not having a presentation at all, you're having a progress meeting. And progress meetings demonstrate only one thing: Unless you've got a finished idea, you haven't made much progress.

You may have whole pages to work in, or you may have smaller spaces; it's never a bad idea to make the ads you pin on the presentation room wall bigger than they will appear in the publication. Acknowledge the fact in your opening sentence by all means, but point out that, since the client is sitting at the boardroom table and the ad is probably 15 feet away from him, the large size is partly to help communicate the idea at that distance.

naked into the conference

If you are producing an idea for a film or television commercial, then always draw up a storyboard. Going into a presentation with only a typewritten script is like going naked to the conference chamber. I know there are arguments that say it's better to act out your commercial rather than draw it. I know it has been said that if you show a woman with blonde hair on the storyboard, the client will want the model in the commercial to have just that hue in her own hair. This is not just naive: It under-estimates the intelligence of the client; if you do think your man is going to react like that, then make it perfectly clear that he is looking at a still drawing, not a piece of live film. A storyboard indicates intent but is never to be interpreted literally. A script is merely words and, although you are perfectly clear what they mean, you're going to have to be a communications wizard to get what you "see" in a script to be the same thing as clients "see." A storyboard is the one occasion when you can be sure that twelve pictures are worth twelve thousand words.

Moreover, when you draw storyboards, you give your work weight. I know that no first-rate agency should have to provide a client with evidence that it has done work. But a storyboard *is* evidence that you have done work, more work than appears on a single typewritten sheet, and evidence helps, even if it's not needed to prove your case. Finally, films and commercials are to do with *pictures*; how can you hope to show them in any light at all if you don't *use* pictures? Bill Bernbach, the best-known copywriter of them all, says: "How can you storyboard a smile?" There's no answer to that. But there is another question: "How can you write a smile in a TV script?" I'll put my money on a professional storyboard artist to communicate the intention quicker.

I have little experience of making test commercials. I've done it, and it's expensive and rarely achieves the effect you want, because you can't buy the right artists or the right director and, until recently, you couldn't edit very efficiently on videotape. I'm not sold on the need to make test commercials: For one thing, they only last half a minute and the client needs something he can look at for a lot longer than that and, if necessary, take away in his briefcase afterwards. So I don't advocate going to all this time, trouble, and expense; it's simply not worth it. But it is worth doing storyboards. I would never ask any creative team to present a commercial without them.

horses for courses

So the first basic principle in a presentation is to arm yourself with the right creative ammunition. Large, well-drawn concepts for press ads and the same large, well-drawn storyboards of the key frames of your film. There are times when it helps to have the whole storyboard up on your easel at once, and other times when it's best to put the key frames up a picture at a time. You will have to decide which method is appropriate for the commercial you have to show; content is all.

If you are a junior copywriter in an agency that has a set formula for presenting creative work, and that formula does not follow the one I have outlined here, then you will obviously have to work within the system that operates at your place. If the agency policy is to keep you away from the client, then you'll have to pass your work over to someone else. If it's your agency's practice to present scripts rather than storyboards, then you'll have to abide by the rules. In that situation, there's no profit in banging your head against the wall. All I would say is that when you get into place that allows you to make your own decisions on matters of presentation, you'll find my advice will pay dividends.

So much for arming yourself with the material you have to present. Now a word about the speech you are going to make. Unless you are highly experienced in the business, it won't do you any harm to make a few notes on what you want to say. What matters is not that you may forget to make some of the points in your sales story, but that you might not make them in the right order. You argument should have simplicity and a logic that is irrefutable, and logic is mostly a matter of the order in which you make your proposition. I'm not suggesting you need a rehearsal every time you prepare for a presentation—though if it is a vitally important one, then that may not be amiss—but simply that you should muster a logical case for what you want to say and support your thesis with as many facts as are relevant.

You have one invaluable aid in creative presentations, apart from the fact that you have a client's undivided attention, that is "the creative strategy." The following story may illustrate how crucial the strategy can be. I once made a very important advertising campaign for a client who was launching a new product. As luck would have it, on the day of the presentation, I was struck down with the flu, so my art director—no slouch in presentations—had to take the job instead. We picked a bad time of the week, Friday afternoon, and we were in the middle of a heat wave.

Result: a lost campaign, not through anybody's fault but through force of circumstance. The agency made a brave decision—to re-present the work a week or so later, taking into account the client's comments and giving due consideration to his objections, which, in my view, were primarily the result of imprecise thinking. Now the decision to re-present is a difficult one at any time, and the chances of success are around 100-to-1 against. But we were sure we had a good campaign and equally sure that it was a sound (not to say imaginative) interpretation of the strategy.

The second meeting with the client began in a tense atmosphere, but I had decided several days before that it was no part of my job to "sell" the client a campaign he had rejected. It was very much part of my job to get him to agree we were working to the right strategy. After all, both agency and client had worked to put it together; all we had to decide was that we'd done the job right, and no circumstance had arisen to force a change. I started my talk by admitting the situation the agency was in; I was not, I said, going to present a new advertising campaign. But I also emphasized that I was not going to try to make the client accept the campaign he had already seen. What I wanted to do was examine the suggestions made at the previous presentation and see whether they could and should be integrated into the strategy. I said at the outset: "Mr. Client, *there is always another campaign.*"

no "psychobabble," please

So we went through our business reasoning, point by point. I had a list of objections that the client had raised, and we examined each of those carefully to see whether there was a place for any of them in the argument we wanted to put to our audience. I was coldly logical, careful to speak simply and avoid jargon, and I used phrases that my wife would have understood if I had been putting the case for the product to her. And I raised the objections to the argument I thought she would raise and then, whenever possible, overcame them with advantages that stemmed from the product and had been outlined in the creative strategy.

The client, since he realised he was not going to be steam-rollered into buying any creative work, was prepared to listen. In not too long a time, we agreed that the thinking outlined in the strategy was sound and that sensible arguments against it could be refuted sensibly. It was only at this point that I turned to the creative work. Again I asked the client to only decide if the ads lived up to the thinking behind the strategy, and I went through the headline and copy claims point by point, cross-checking against the strategy to see that nothing had been missed, nothing understated, and, equally important, nothing overstated. Because the strategy was demonstrably right, it was a reasonably simple job to demonstrate that the ads were right. They were not the only way to skin the cat (and I was careful to make that point too); but they were a highly professional interpretation of a sound selling proposition, had not been arrived at lightly, and, if we were to go back to the drawing board, it wasn't because we were off strategy, but because the client—entirely within his rights—simply didn't like the work.

In meetings of this kind it is important to admit that you may not be 100 percent right; you shouldn't expect to win every point in every argument; clients are very rarely fools, and unless you have done a great deal of homework, they probably know more about the product and certainly more about the manufacturing and distribution problems than you. There is a postscript to this story. When the advertisements finally ran, they pushed the client's product to number one in the market. And although he no longer works with the product in question, nor I with the agency in question, we still greet each other on Christian name terms.

think like a creative person, talk like an accountant

You can take it from me that any attempt to point out the beauty, "creativity," or impact of the ads would have been quite useless. No client is impressed with those qualities if he doesn't like the big idea. But once the suspicion of high-pressure salesmanship has been set at rest, and you have the client's ear, business sense normally prevails. You can't expect a client to recognize a brilliant advertising campaign when he sees it (What is brilliant, anyway? What one man loves another won't buy at any price), and it's not his job to know good work when he sees it.

It's your job to convince him that the work is good, and you won't do that simply by declaring, "Look at this; isn't it great?" That is why it is vital that the creative team are involved when the strategy is written and that they understand it and agree with it. And also that they look on it not as a restriction of their imagination but as a discipline that will point them in only one direction in which good solutions are to be found. So the moral is this: You should go into a client presentation determined to *prove that the ads are "on strategy."* And the imagination and craft with which they interpret that strategy should speak for themselves. Never go to the wall over a campaign; it isn't worth it, and anyway, in the last analysis, the client has the right to say, "I don't like it." But by all means do your utmost to defend the strategy. That is easier because the client has had a major say in devising it, and moreover, if the strategy is correct, you can always find another way to interpret it. (I shall have more to say about the idea that there is always another campaign in Chapter 15.)

think while you listen

When you have made your presentation and ads are on the wall waiting for the client's comments, then is the time you have to be able to think on your feet. First presentations should be concerned with concepts; it's rarely a good idea to get down to discussing the body text at this early stage. Get your pictures and headlines agreed; show that each different ad is making a single point in the selling pitch and that, together, the ads make up an attractive and coherent personality for the product. Since the work you have done probably took several weeks to perfect, and since each ad has been given several "overnight tests," you will have already mustered your reasons for why you did what you did. The time to expand on them is if you have to face heavy criticism; but be careful to deal with your client in an attitude of friendliness. Be prepared to listen and—if it doesn't hurt the campaign—within reason, to agree. I cannot emphasize too strongly that the best defense is common sense and logic. The worst situation to be in is defending an ad for emotional reasons or because, at that moment, you can't think of another way of doing it. This is not a plea for compromise. I am very wary of the desire to accommodate every point the client makes as soon as he makes it, because often he is simply asking questions to find out whether you have thought the business through and found the right answers.

surprise, surprise

A client who cross-examines you in a presentation can soon fathom how much thinking you have done on the campaign and how deeply you are committed to the ads. He can also tell very quickly if you are defending work for the wrong reasons, and if you are not as confident of your recommendations as you would like to appear. Vibes come over in client meetings; the rights and wrongs of an argument will soon become apparent if discussions are held in an atmosphere of businesslike common sense, with no allowances made for creative temperament. (Which is not to say the client shouldn't make allowances for unexpected turns of phrase in headlines and suprises in the ads.) If I come out of a presentation without having surprised my client with my creative work, I think I've failed.

leave at the right time

Let us say that at the end of the presentation the client has given the tentative "yes" and that the ads seem to have jumped the first hurdle on their way to the medium in which they'll appear. That's the time to stop. A highly successful account person I know puts the situation in six words: "Make the sale. And get out." Once the decision to accept the work has been made, any further discussion is generally unprofitable. People are tired, get bogged down in unimportant details, and can often forget the original intent of the work. The initial surprise of seeing the ads has gone, the client's attention is no longer yours for the asking, and prolonged discussion simply raises doubts and second thoughts. Remember, the first impression is the important thing: The average reader will give your ad about 1½ seconds, so there's little to be gained by poring over your work for 1½ hours. Make sure you know what you and the client agree on, what you disagree on, and the next steps to take. Then go, man, go.

15

How to Live
with a
Dead Campaign

In theory, there should be only three reasons for a client to reject a campaign:

1. It's not "on strategy."

2. Events have overtaken it.

3. It's been done before.

In practice, we can add a fourth reason that, although it may seem irrational, is, in my view, perfectly acceptable.

4. The client doesn't like it.

As far as the first reason is concerned—the campaign that doesn't give a correct interpretation of the strategy—this should have been killed in the creative director's office, or certainly a long time before it got presented to the client. There is absolutely no value in the agency people and the client agreeing on a strategy if the creative people don't follow it. And consequently, there is no way to defend it during a presentation, and it ought to be killed there and then.

If events overtake your campaign, the fault can lie in several places: One is with the client, since he may not have apprised the agency of the new situation; another is with the account people, who may have known that something had happened, but either didn't pass on the information to the writer and art director or assumed that it would make no difference.

If the campaign has been done before, either by your own client or by a competitor again it should die, or the client will simply be spending his money to promote someone else's products. But it can often happen that nobody knows of the existence of the other campaign (it is not unknown for two agencies to produce similar advertisements, almost simultaneously), in which case you have to accept the fact that duplication can happen.

You are best advised to give up your version and start again; if two people think of the same idea at the same time, there is a likelihood that it's a pretty obvious idea, and you will be the stronger of the two agencies if you volunteer to rethink. A client shouldn't be too hard on his agency if it does produce work similar to someone else—provided he is sure he is dealing with a first-rate agency. Creative people in the best shops strongly dislike "cribbing" and are far too conscientious to present another agency's thinking as their own.

the illogical "no"

Which brings us to the forth reason—the client doesn't like it. I may have surprised you when I said I felt this reason to be acceptable. I believe this because, in the last analysis, the client is paying the bill and should not be forced into buying a product he doesn't feel happy with—you would never buy anything you didn't like. But more than this, even if a clever account person does persuade the client to accept work that he dislikes, and even if that work appears in the media, the client will always have a deep-down feeling he has been pressured, and that is the first step to looking for a new agency. One thing is virtually certain: Even if the work runs for a year, it will certainly be killed at the end of that time anyway (disappointed clients can be very persistent) unless it has proved, beyond any doubt, to be effective.

If your client does say "no" and cannot articulate his reasons, some agencies offer to "research" the campaign to prove that it is right. The proper place for research, however, is before the campaign has been written. That way, all the findings, based on only the proposition, can be included in the finished work. Campaigns researched after they have been done are more often than not going to take a beating. (We all know how research groups like to set themselves up as advertising judges.) And anyway, even if everything does go the way the agency wants, if I were a client and I hated the work, I would politely suggest that the agency stuff the research findings. So what should the disappointed creative person do? What certainly *doesn't* help is to blow your top. I have done it myself after a disastrous presentation, and it is simply sound and fury, signifying nothing.

oh, it's you again!

You must always remember that you are going to have to meet the client again. You are going to have to present him with a second campaign. If you prove yourself insensitive to his feelings and seemingly unable to accept his views, he will only give you a hard time the second time around. The best relationship between creative people and a client is that of "friends." You have to show that you understand his business problems, his likes and dislikes, and his "intuitive" feelings on how his product should be promoted. He may never be able to produce a campaign himself, but do remember that he has had the entrepreneurial skills to devise and manufacture a product, secure distribution for it, and find enough money to advertise it. Not many genuine entrepreneurs are clowns; they very often have a knack of being able to sell five-cent apples for ten cents, which is a skill most copywriters could well do with. So, above all, try to retain a good relationship with your client; convince him that you are on his side and that you both want the best possible advertising for the product. Some creative people are in the unhappy position of having earned themselves reputations for being hard to get along with when criticized; in the final event, this can only lead to the client telling the agency that he wants a completely new group to work on his account.

listen to what he means

The most positive thing you can do is spend time talking with the client, face to face. If possible, try not to let the account people get in the way. If you listen carefully to what your man says and then take out of the meeting what he actually means (which are rarely one and the same thing), you will be in a better position to have a second try. I have known a time when I did work for a client that was rejected not once, but three times; finally, I sat down and had a real heart-to-heart talk with him, not in an atmosphere of rancor but of cooperation. At the end of that talk, what he wanted was crystal clear, and then my only responsibility was to put it down on paper in a way that was truly professional. Don't get me wrong; I'm not saying give the client what he *says* he wants; instead, listen to what he says and use your skill and experience to turn those thoughts into good advertisements.

Clients rarely know how to make good ads. But they are not without ideas on what sells their product, and many of them may have been out on the road actually doing the selling, so take care before you reject what they have learned from that experience.

clients lose sleep too

At the same time, it is not uncommon for clients to be so close to their products that they can't separate sales points from simple information. They want you to understand the sleepless nights they have had thinking about the product in all its facets, and this can frequently get them bogged down in detail. They ask to have every single advantage in the headline repeated in the subheading and reiterated throughout the body copy. You can combat this if you remember two things. First, the experience of the tire manufacturer who, although he had a terrific number of sales points to make, honed them down to one main thought: safety. Always try to make an ad that concentrates at first on a main thought. Second, there is a little rhyme that helps you and your client to see details more clearly:

> *Oh tell me this, and tell me true*
> *Or else, my love, to hell with you,*
> *Less how the product came to be*
> *And more for what it does for me.*

Sad to say, the customer does not want to know the history of the product and all the problems the client had before he perfected it. He wants to know what's in it for him. Say that little ditty to your client (nicely, of course) and it will help you to make it clear to him the importance of promise, promise, and more promise, which is (as you've probably heard a million times) the soul of an advertisement.

OK, your campaign has been killed, but your relationship with the client hasn't; in fact, if you've done your talking well, it's on a better footing than it ever has been, and you are beginning to get a "feel" of his expectations (and, indeed, his limitations). What's the next move?

new doesn't mean
once more with feeling

Throw out of your mind all the thoughts of the first campaign. I don't mean forget the market background—far from it. All the time spend finding out facts about the product, the buyer, and the market is time very well invested, and it will pay you dividends now. But don't try to produce the same creative work with different words, because if the client doesn't like the proposition the first time around, he surely won't like the same idea expressed differently. And anyway, if you're any good, you found the best words to use for your first campaign. You must look for a new idea. How?

Every good agency has one or two people in the creative department who won't mind helping. The first person is, of course, the creative director, and if he is any good at all, he will have brought his mind to bear on your problem and be able to make some suggestions, even if they are only tentative and not formed into a campaign idea. But go to all the senior people in the creative department and talk things over. Listen to people who are positive. It may be that this is your first campaign on a product that has been transferred to you from another group. Go to the people who previously did the good work; they will not mind you picking their brains; if they have the right attitude to our business, they should be flattered. But if you meet someone who tells you not to be surprised that your work has been turned down and who goes on to talk about what a rotten product you've got and what a difficult company you have to deal with, the best thing to do is switch off or change the subject. All they are trying to do is make excuses for shoddy work *they've* done; complaints about products and clients can only dishearten you, and since you are going to have to go into the arena a second time you would be well advised to enter with good grace. Seek out the good thinkers in your agency, people not afraid to make suggestions on how to approach the problem, and even if they don't actually have an idea for you, they may say a sentence or two that sets you thinking on a new line.

talk to the media people

Take a fresh look at the media you are using and, if it's at all practical, change it. Good advice for every creative person is to have a special buddy in the media department.

You get a hold of him and tell him who you want to talk to and how much money you've got to spend. Say the target audience is young girls, aged 16–24, and the campaign you've had rejected used whole pages in the right women's magazines. He may have news of a different kind of space the magazines are promoting at that time—say, the mini-page, or four quarter-pages across the spread. Any suggestion of a different way to reach the audience can be very helpful when you are considering a new approach to creative work. If he becomes interested in the creative job and understands that media buying is really part of the creative function, a good media man will never leave you without at least having stimulated your mind as to possible new ways to approach your campaign. I will go further and say you should never produce any major campaign without first having a long talk with someone in the media department. I have always been lucky enough to strike up a relationship with one particular guy who never minds using his imagination and isn't mesmerised by cost-per-thousands. If you can't find a good friend among the media people, at least you can get together with the planners on each of your accounts as the opportunities arise.

don't get whipped by the clock

So you have talked the situation over with the creative director, you have walked around picking the best brains available, and you have had a pow-wow with the media guys. Your next problem will probably be time. Since your first campaign was produced to meet copy dates, it's likely that these will not be far away. Worries about deadlines never help you do good work. So, if possible, you should try to get extensions on your first copy dates; it might even not do too much harm if the launch date is postponed for a few days to ensure the creative work is right. If you spend a million dollars on a second-rate campaign, you won't have proved a great deal just by launching on the day planned.

Clients understand this too, and account people certainly should be sympathetic. I'm not saying ask for more time on principle; but I am saying it's never good to be whipped by the clock. Parkinson's law certainly applies in creative departments, as it does in any office, and I know a number of good creative people who are at their best when the pressure is on. But if lack of time worries you, then it is a handicap the rest of the agency should do their utmost to remove. The man with the most authority to help here is the creative director, so if deadlines are ridiculous, put your case to him.

remember robert-the-bruce

Now, a word of warning. There can be a temptation, especially among those creative people who have had little experience in the business, to try less hard the second time around. I'm not saying it applies to everyone, but the disappointment of a rejected campaign can linger for days and kill enthusiasm. If you give in and produce second-rate work, you'll be asking for trouble. The creative director should kick you around the building, but you will also upset your account people, and you will get no sympathy whatsoever from the experienced creative people who will have been in your situation and *worked* to get out of it. But let us for a moment suppose that you *do* manage to get some second-rate ad through the system. No one will be sorrier than yourself in the days to come when the proofs roll off the presses or the commercial appears and you blush every time someone puts your name to it. What's worse, all the efforts you put into the first campaign, and the tears you shed over the second, will never show in the ads that finally appear. To the great Public, not to mention your co-workers in the trade, it will look like just another low-class job where nobody tried hard enough. And this is precisely what it will be. Whenever a creative person opens his portfolio and shows me a poor ad, but hurries on to tell me I should have seen the original (but the client didn't like it!), I know exactly what to think.

There is another temptation: to quit! You decide you're not appreciated in your present agency so you'll go somewhere else.

You either call up your favorite head-hunter and tell him you're looking, or you start to scan the employment pages of the trade press. This state of affairs—quite funny when you read about it, but believe me, it really happens—can go on until you get too high up to run away; is it an answer? In my experience, not really, since it is a fact of life that problems you turn your back on have this unfortunate knack of turning up again from another direction. And not just in agency life. I am sure there are plenty of clients who think twice about swopping agencies (and hence gutsy creative people) because the devil they know is better than the devil they haven't met yet. Certainly I am sure that the client whose expectations you know is 20 times better than the client whose expectations *you* haven't had to meet yet. This is not to say you have to become a punching bag, but hopefully you're too intelligent for that anyway. Move on when the right opportunity presents itself by all means, but there's no profit in changing agencies as an escape route. The number of people who change their jobs for the right reasons is small in any business, but you can do yourself a big favor if you look very carefully before you leap. There is a very strong possibility—I'd say you can almost bet on it—that the first account you have to work on at your new place will present you with the same kind of problems you refused to face at your old place. And this isn't the fault of advertising agencies, it's the very nature of business—any business—and, you might say, of life itself.

an idea to remember

So, to summarize: Don't burn your boats with the client; listen carefully to what he has to say; fillet the meat out of his suggestions; talk with your creative director and the other helpful creative people you have around; reconsider your choice of media; never try to regurgitate your old work; do your utmost to see you have enough time; don't give up and produce poor work; and don't take the easy route to another agency. Try, if you can, to bear this next thought in mind. It is not a popular idea, and there are some places where they don't like it to get around for fear the client will start whipping the agency. But it is perfectly true, and if you can weave it into your working philosophy you will find you walk with a lighter step.

The thought is this: *There is always another campaign.* I could make it stronger and say there is always another campaign inside you, but as sure as God made little fishes, if you can't think of it, someone else in or outside your agency certainly can. So be professional about it; that is the truth of this whole situation; accept it and live up to it; and no one will ever get the better of you.

Which brings me to some thoughts on what a professional creative person should be. I have a view, as this books testifies, that the true advertising writer is one who has taken time and trouble to learn his skills. Not just through practice, but through study. By this, I don't advocate that you spend long years in college. I would never have a creative person spend more than one scholastic year getting the foundations of his craft, and if he can spend that year going around the other departments in an agency rather than at college, so much the better. When you get to the stage where you are making and presenting big campaigns for major clients (and I don't see this happening until several years after you first start as a copywriter) then your behavior should be such that can only win you respect in the eyes of your client. He should be able to view you with the same confidence and expect to hear you speak with the same authority as the marketing man with his computer print-outs and the research man with his depth interviews. You should have a grasp of the market situation on a par with the account person who makes the selling recommendations; put in the vernacular, that means you should understand buying and selling. You buy cheap, you put labor into the product, and you sell at the best price the market will bear. And you do that for one reason only: to make a profit. You should not see yourself as a frustrated poet or novelist who prostitutes his art by writing copy. Write poetry by all means, but put the same craft into your ads; earn your living honestly. Realize that your function is to get people to spend, and help your client to earn his living and keep his factories busy and his employees rich.

Accept that you are in the engine room of the agency, making the only product the public will see, and never be afraid to roll your sleeves up and get sweaty. Some people will say you work in an ivory tower, but this is no more true of you than it is of your client, who also works in an office with pleasant furniture and, maybe, a carpet on the floor yet has to keep his job by making goods that the public want. Ivory tower critics invariably live in ivory towers themselves; that's where they get the idea from. Since you are part of the cycle of production, there is not place in your job for temperament or displays of heavy sighing. Shout and scream in your own office by all means, set fire to the layouts, rush home, kick the dog, and beat the wife. That's expected from creative people—just don't do it where anyone else has to suffer it.

If you have decided you want to be a creative person, behave so that you can be justly proud of the work you do, whether it's the first campaign for the product or (God forbid) the fourth. A true test is whether you are pleased to have you name connected with it if it should ever come under discussion. If you always make good ads, you won't just have an enviable portfolio to show. You will have clients who look forward to presentations from you and are keen to buy your work if they possibly can. You will have account people who ask your opinion on matters of marketing, expect you to make a major contribution to any strategy you draw up together, and want to have you working for their clients. Because you are professional, and are recognized as such, you will soon be able to command a good salary, which will increase just as long as you produce outstanding creative work. And if all this is true, it need not be too long before you begin win advertising awards and earn yourself a name. Love, security, wealth, and recognition. What else is there?

Index